Photograph by Fenton Kremer for Big White House Winery page 153

Signature
WINES & WINERIES
OF COASTAL CALIFORNIA

Donati Family Vineyard, page 55

Noteworthy Wines From
Leading Estate and Boutique Wineries
on California's Central Coast

Published by Intermedia Publishing Services
Dallas, TX (972) 898-8915

Published by

Intermedia Publishing Services, Inc
5815 Richwater Drive
Dallas, TX 75232
972-898-8915
www.panache.com

Publisher: Brian G. Carabet
Regional Publisher: Marc Zurba
Managing Editor: Katrina Autem
Currator and Writer: Mira Honeycutt
Art Director: Adam Carabet
Administrative Coordinator: Vicki Martin

Printed in Malaysia

Distributed by Independent Publishers Group
800.888.4741

PUBLISHER'S DATA

SIGNATURE WINES & WINERIES OF COASTAL CALIFORNIA

Library of Congress Control Number: 2019952922

ISBN: 978-0-9969653-9-2

First Printing 2020

10 9 8 7 6 5 4 3 2 1

Signature
WINES & WINERIES
OF COASTAL CALIFORNIA

Noteworthy Wines From Leading Estate and Boutique Wineries
on California's Central Coast

Opolo Vineyards, page 89

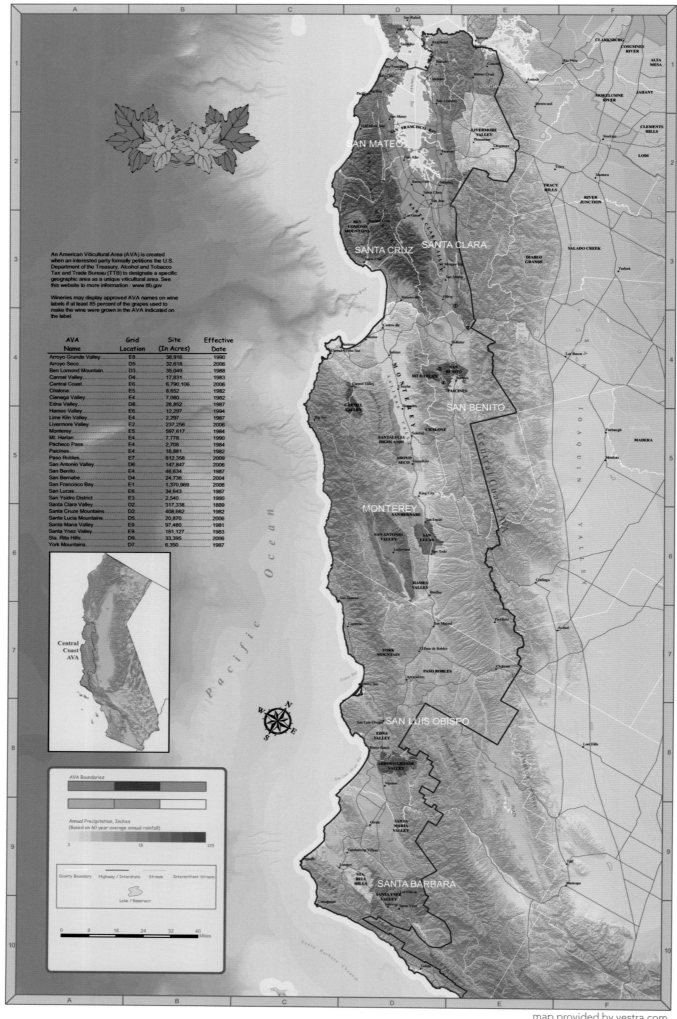

An American Viticultural Area (AVA) is created when an interested party formally petitions the U.S. Department of the Treasury, Alcohol and Tobacco Tax and Trade Bureau (TTB) to designate a specific geographic area as a unique viticultural area. See this website to more information : www.ttb.gov

Wineries may display approved AVA names on wine labels if at least 85 percent of the grapes used to make the wine were grown in the AVA indicated on the label.

AVA Name	Grid Location	Site (In Acres)	Effective Date
Arroyo Grande Valley	E8	38,916	1990
Arroyo Seco	D5	32,618	2006
Ben Lomond Mountain	D3	35,049	1988
Carmel Valley	D4	17,831	1983
Central Coast	E6	6,790,106	2006
Chalone	E5	8,652	1982
Cienega Valley	E4	7,080	1982
Edna Valley	D8	28,852	1987
Hames Valley	E6	12,297	1994
Lime Kiln Valley	E4	2,297	1987
Livermore Valley	E2	237,256	2006
Monterey	E5	597,617	1984
Mt. Harlan	E4	7,778	1990
Pacheco Pass	E4	2,708	1984
Paicines	E4	18,881	1982
Paso Robles	E7	612,358	2009
San Antonio Valley	D6	147,847	2006
San Benito	E4	46,634	1987
San Bernabe	D4	24,736	2004
San Francisco Bay	E1	1,370,969	2006
San Lucas	E6	34,643	1987
San Ysidro District	E3	2,540	1990
Santa Clara Valley	D2	317,338	1989
Santa Cruze Mountains	D2	408,662	1982
Santa Lucia Mountains	D5	20,870	2006
Santa Maria Valley	E9	97,480	1981
Santa Ynez Valley	E9	181,127	1983
Sta. Rita Hills	D9	33,395	2006
York Mountains	D7	6,350	1987

Central Coast AVA

AVA Boundaries

Annual Precipitation, Inches
(Based on 60 year average annual rainfall)

2   18   125

County Boundary   Highway / Interstate   Stream   Intermittent Stream

Lake / Reservoir

0   8   16   24   32   40
Miles

map provided by vestra.com

INTRODUCTION

J. Lohr Vineyards, page 65

The wine region of California's Central Coast cuts a wide swath, meandering from Santa Barbara County in the south to San Francisco Bay in the north. The 300-mile-route is framed by the Pacific Ocean to the west and the towering Sierra Madre Mountains and the Padres National Forest to the east. Stretching along El Camino Royal (the royal route harking back to the Spanish settlers now largely Highway 101), the scenic route snakes through oak-studded hillsides and old stagecoach routes then winds back to a spectacular coastline. The region is deeply rooted in the lore of early California from Native Chumash Indians and the Old West tales of Yankee ranchers, settlers, and soldiers to Franciscan monks and Spanish land-grant rancheros. In fact, it was Father Junipero Serra who planted more than 1,000 vines in 1797 at the historic Mission San Miguel Arcangel near Paso Robles.

What's so special about the Central Coast wine region is its diversity. There are multiple macro and microclimates, vast variations in soils, and extreme diurnal temperature swings. Vineyard plantings can stretch from fertile valley floors to elevations of 2,500 feet above sea level. This diversity draws maverick winemakers who love to experiment with more than 40 varieties of wine grapes grown in the area. The result is a broad variation of wines produced throughout this region, with each AVA (American Viticultural Area) presenting its own distinctive flavor profile.

Santa Barbara County's wine trails meander through hamlets such as Santa Ynez, Los Alamos, Los Olivos, Ballard Canyon, and Buellton. There are various sub-appellations anchored in these small towns, defining the area's terroir, so for example, Chardonnay and Pinot Noir from Santa Rita Hills AVA stretching from Buellton to Lompoc will be distinctly different from a Chardonnay in the Santa Maria Valley AVA. The same goes for varietals like Syrah, which will present a different flavor profile coming from the warmer Ballard Canyon AVA than from, say, cooler Santa Rita Hills.

Écluse Wines, page 61

Seven Oxen Winery, page 109

Anchored midway between Los Angeles and San Francisco, Paso Robles AVA offers a completely different portfolio of wines because of its inland location and extreme triple-digit summer heat. This is where Bordeaux and Rhône varietals rule. The area's terroir is unique, offering more than 30 different types of soil series from calcareous to granites and volcanic. Paso's 11 sub-appellations are spread throughout 40,000 acres of vineyards that stretch 42 miles east to west and 32 miles north to south. While Cabernet Sauvignon is the most widely planted varietal, Paso is known for its big bold reds, blending Bordeaux and Rhöne-style grapes to produce what has become the distinctive Paso Blend. The region's heritage Zinfandel grape often finds its way into these "muscle-flexing" blends that can, at times, include more than eight different varietals. However, due to its diversity, Paso can also grow some remarkable Italian and Spanish varietals such as Sangiovese, Tempranillo, and Garnacha.

Further up north, Monterey County's cool coastal region along the Santa Lucia Highlands prides itself in exceptional Chardonnay and Pinot Noir. On the eastern side, the warmer Carmel Valley area produces full-bodied Bordeaux varietals. The Central Coast region is also home to off-the-beaten path wineries ensconced in the steep mountain topography of Santa Cruz Mountains and along Santa Clara Valley, also known as Silicon Valley.

Vina Robles, page 125

Aleksander Wine, page 13

Brochelle Vineyards, page 31

Murrietta's Well, page 171

This book covers Livermore Valley, located about 35 miles east of San Francisco and regarded as one of the oldest wine regions in the state. This is where the historic Wente family propagated the Chardonnay clone, which became the genetic source of 80 percent of Chardonnay vines in California.

California's wine industry continues to make a sizable impact on the U.S. economy and its global image. As per the Wine Institute's current report, California is America's number-one wine state and the fourth largest producer in the world and accounts for more than 95 percent of U.S. wine exports. The state is home to 139 AVAs, scattered around some 637,000 acres of vineyards, where more than 110 wine grape varieties are planted that contribute to 4.28 million tons of grapes. With so much to offer, it's no wonder that the state attracts upwards of 24 million tourists to the wineries annually, generating $4.2 billion in annual tourism expenditures.

This book presents a comprehensive insight in the region's wine trails, chronicling the finest estate and boutique wineries and their passionate winemakers. We hope you enjoy the Central Coast wine experience.

Mira Advani Honeycutt

Mira Advani Honeycutt
Content Curator

Calipaso Winery & Villa, page 37

Wente Vineyards, page 183

SOUTHERN REGION

San Luis Obispo County

Santa Barbara County

Red Soles Winery, page 99

CONTENTS

NORTHERN REGION

Villa San Juilette, page 117

9

Derby Wine Estates, page 47

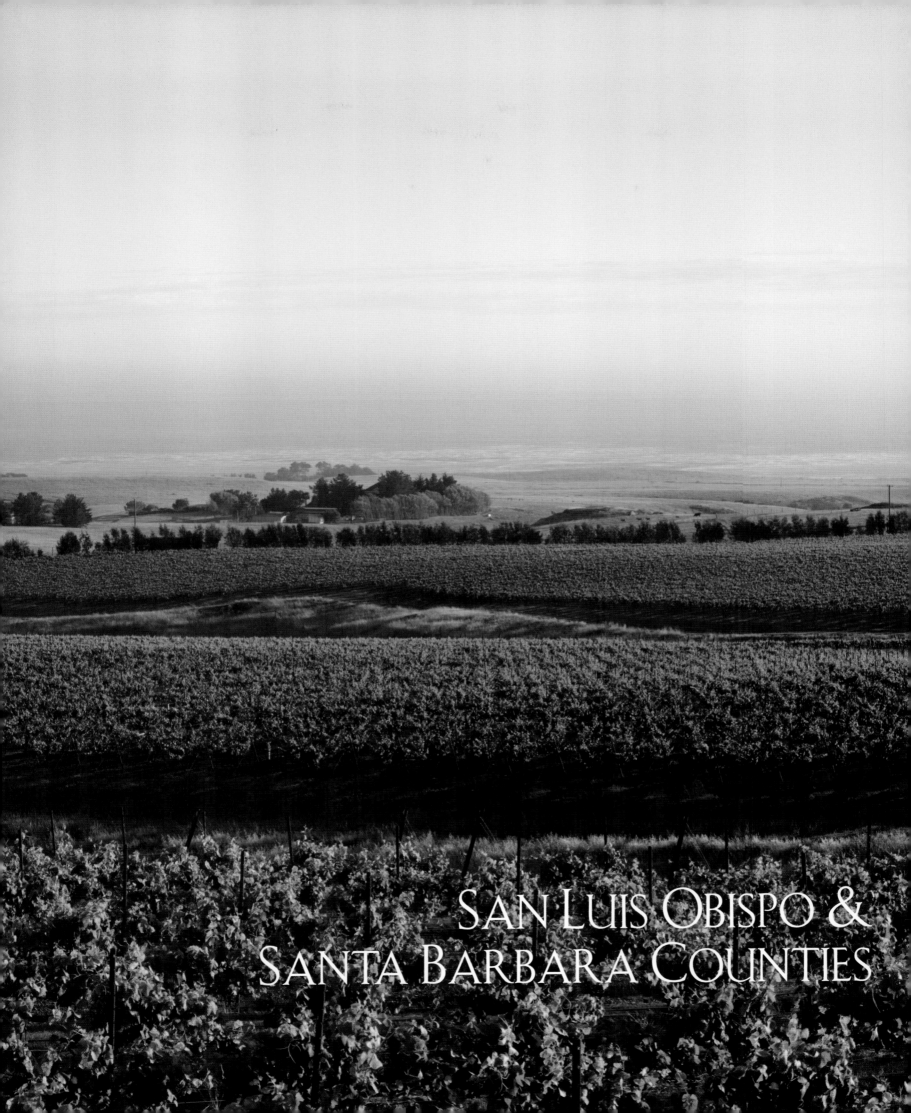

SAN LUIS OBISPO &
SANTA BARBARA COUNTIES

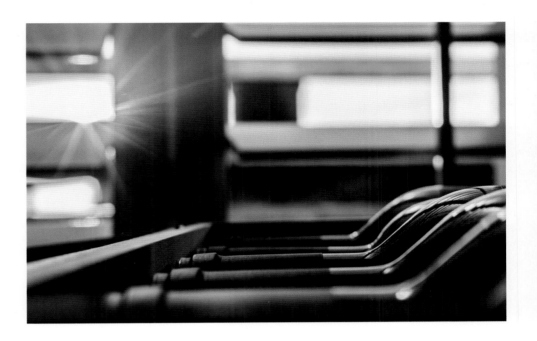

Aleksander Wine by S&G Estate PASO ROBLES

If passion and commitment had a flavor, they would most certainly taste like Aleksander Wine. The winery was built on a dedication to excellence, and a pure love of winemaking is apparent in every bottle.

Aleksander was started by Aleksander "Sasha" Vujacic, a two-time NBA Champion with the Los Angeles Lakers, and his family. He began cultivating his love of wine during the early stages of his career in Italy alongside his father, Goran. They set out on a mission to fulfill their dream of finding a small parcel of well-situated land, where they would establish a family winery and integrate their passion and knowledge of European winemaking to produce a unique Bordeaux-style blend. They wanted to bring together European and Californian characteristics.

Set in the El Pomar region of Paso Robles, Aleksander's grapes are grown on S&G Estate, a 30-acre parcel purchased by the family in 2009. Home to more than 600 Mission olive trees and 13 acres of Bordeaux varietal vineyards, the estate is nestled within the slopes of the region and is known for its calcareous soil and Templeton gap breezes. These conditions are ideal for the seven acres of Merlot, three acres of Cabernet Sauvignon, and one acre of Malbec, Cabernet Franc, and Petit Verdot each—all used to produce Aleksander Wine.

FACING PAGE: The S&G Estate Oak Tree is more than 350 years old. Its strong roots remind us to cherish our own.

TOP: The S & G Estate Wine Cellar holds up to 1,000 bottles.
Photographs by Alex Cvetkov

The property includes a fully operational winery, a humidified barrel room, private tasting room and a pizza oven for private winemaker dinners and family gatherings. Along with the winery, the property is also home to a working olive oil production facility where the family produces award-winning extra virgin olive oil. Wine production includes a luxury red wine blend reminiscent of the great wines of Bordeaux. Centered around Merlot, it has varying degrees of contribution from other classic Bordeaux grapes, depending on the vintage.

Contributing to the complexity of the wines are the French, Serbian and Eastern European oak barrels in which Aleksander wines are aged for a minimum of 18 months and the Reserves a minimum of 24. After bottling, the wine is aged in-bottle for at least 10 months prior to release. Both labels are full-bodied and aromatic, perfectly balanced with rich, dark fruit, and a silky tannin texture.

The soils, drainage and temperature variation in the southeastern corner of Paso Robles combine to form the ideal terroir to give life to these rich and supple wines, whose character is accentuated by the carefully-selected barrels. Annual yields produce approximately 35 tons of grapes which equates to 2,300 cases.

TOP: The vibrant private tasting room on the family's Paso Robles property is reserved for members of the Aleksander Wine Club.

BELOW: These intricate hand-carved doors open to welcome members to Aleksander's charming tasting room.
Photographs by Alex Cvetkov

2012 ALEKSANDER RESERVE

GOURMET PAIRINGS

Serve this wine with grilled lamb chops and other grilled meats, such as filet mignon, ribeye, and even pork chops.

TASTING NOTES

A clean medium-dark hue and a charming earthy fragrance with hints of violet distinguish the 2012 Aleksander Reserve. There are notes of dark chocolate, roasted nuts, and black coffee, but no sweetness except for notes of blackberry, and silky tannins on the finish.

WINEMAKER'S INSIGHT

The 2012 Aleksander Reserve is the first vintage to embody the estate-grown Cabernet Franc and Petit Verdot. Each varietal was aged separately for a year. Following this aging period, the varietals were blended and aged until the wine reached the optimal structure and balance.

TECHNICAL DATA

APPELLATION: Paso Robles, CA
COMPOSITION: 55% Merlot, 22% Cabernet Sauvignon, 15% Cabernet Franc, 8% Petit Verdot
MATURATION: Aged 28 months in special barrel selection
CELLARING: Delicious now, but can be cellared for up to 15-20 years

ORDER OUR WINE

Buy our wines by scanning the image on left.

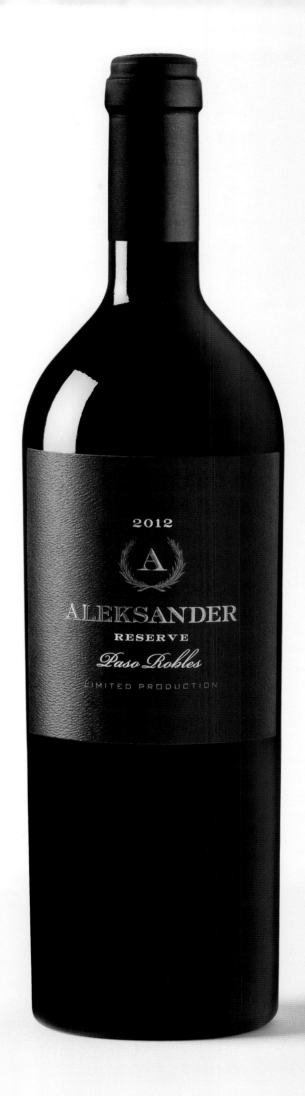

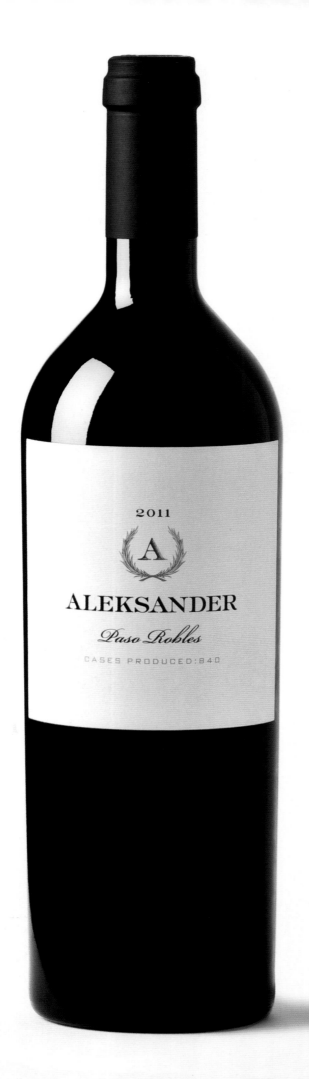

2011 ALEKSANDER

GOURMET PAIRINGS

This wine pairs well with a truffle risotto, or a variety of other rich, mushroom-inspired dishes. Other great choices include a sirloin-tip side steak and grilled vegetables or a hearty beef stew.

TASTING NOTES

The 2011 Aleksander follows a refined yet muscular inaugural 2010 vintage with a modest and elegant presentation of the classic Merlot and Cabernet Sauvignon marriage. A cooler growing season delivered moderate alcohol content, making this wine a nice partner for pairing with a wide variety of dishes.

WINEMAKER'S INSIGHT

The majority of fermentation was done in half-ton bins, punched down three times a day. Merlot and Cabernet Sauvignon were aged separately in a combination of French, Eastern European, and Serbian oak barrels for about a year. Then, the wines were carefully blended to reflect the winemaker's palette, and returned to barrel to age together for an additional six to eight months in a special barrel selection.

AWARDS & DISTINCTIONS

90 points – Antonio Galloni Vinous
91 points – Boozehounds, Michael Cervin
90 points – Connoisseurs' Guide to California Wine
90 points – The Tasting Panel
95 points – *Wine Enthusiast*

TECHNICAL DATA

APPELLATION: Paso Robles
COMPOSITION: 80% Merlot, 20% Cabernet Sauvignon
MATURATION: Aged 24 months in French, Serbian, and Eastern European oak barrels.
CELLARING: Delicious now, with cellaring up to 10-15 years.

LEARN MORE

Visit our website by scanning the image on left.

Two Aleksander Bordeaux-style blends are produced each year: a white label and a black label Reserve. The white label wines amount to nearly 80 percent of the annual production, while the more limited production Reserve makes up the remaining 20 percent. The two labels differ in varietal composition, special barrel selection, and aging period.

With varying additions of Bordeaux varietals, the Merlot-based wines may have Cabernet Sauvignon, Cabernet Franc, Malbec, and Petit Verdot. While forming the blend each year, both yield and grape quality are taken into account. This ensures they reach their goal of crafting an elegant Old World wine with the beauty and intricacy of today.

What is the best way to experience Aleksander wine? Join the Aleksander family. The Wine Club consists of two annual shipments of two bottles each, with a discount, plus priority access to the newest releases. Customized orders are also available. Additional perks include further discounts, a private wine tasting, intimate tours, and exclusive barrel tastings of upcoming wines.

TOP: Our barrel-aging facility has a capacity of 250 barrels with room-temperature conditions ranging between 55-57°F, and a relative humidity between 70-80 percent.

BELOW: A starry sky above our barrel-aging facility.
Photographs by Alex Cvetkov

Allegretto Vineyard Resort PASO ROBLES

The Allegretto Vineyard Resort is an inspiring, joyful, and inclusive place where guests engage in exceptional experiences, spaces, services, and amenities. This is the vision of Douglas Ayres, a keen observer of cultures and traditions, whose affection for humanity and its quest for the divine manifests in each design choice—from the specific architectural footprint, measurements, and ratios of sacred geometry, to the color and tone of each light bulb.

This passion plays out in the art and ancient artifacts that fill the hallways and gardens, reflecting multiple cultures and faiths that serve as windows into the human experience.

Ayres grew up in Newport Beach and studied religion and music at the University of Southern California before embarking on a busy career in sound recording and design prior to joining the family business.

While many accommodations offer guests a physical and mental escape, Allegretto focuses on emotional and spiritual rest. The concept of harmony weaves through the entire property via the abundance of spiritual art and antiques. For example, the driveway has a large rose-compass fountain that welcomes guests, and the lobby features an impressive chandelier hung from a painted ceiling that represents light from heaven; and the Sequoia Room is anchored by a Gothic hearth and displays an imposing cross-section of a felled 214 BC. Sequoia tree. Lavender-scented pathways lead to Via Verona adorned with statues representing some of the world's sacred traditions, among them are Ganesh, bodhisattva Guan Yin, and the Virgin of Guadalupe.

FACING PAGE: Tannat Vineyard on the east side of Allegretto Vineyard Resort with a view of the Bell Tower and the Abbey.
Photograph courtesy of Allegretto Vineyard Resort

ABOVE: Proprietor Douglas Ayres and winemaker Alan Kinne in the barrel room.
Photograph by Sarah Kathleen Photography

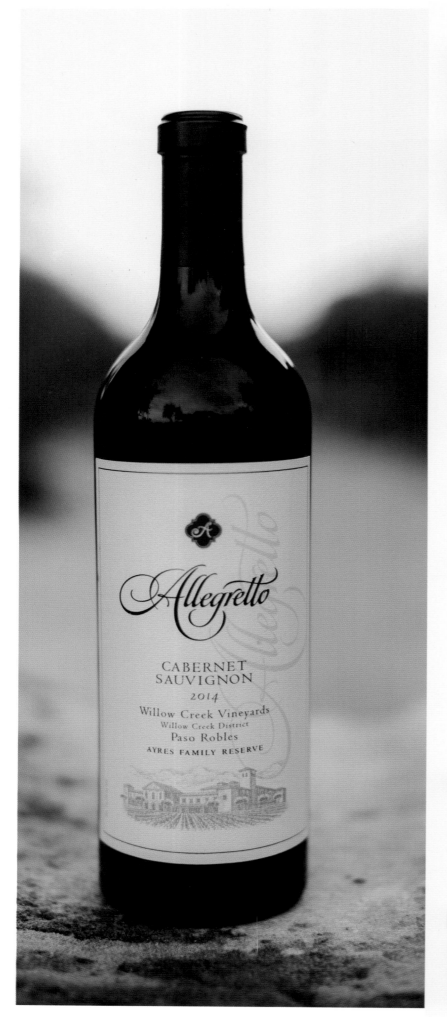

CABERNET SAUVIGNON

GOURMET PAIRINGS
Pair with prime black angus ribeye, roasted carrot nage, asparagus tips, and duck-fat braised purple Peruvian potatoes.

TASTING NOTES
Moderately fruit forward, this wine is big and bold, filled with savory notes. Opulent layers of black currants, wild blackberries, and green peppercorn carry through to the palate, which is accented by firm tannins and a rich mouth feel. A long lingering, velvety finish is reminiscent of an aged, first-growth Bordeaux.

WINEMAKER'S INSIGHT
The grapes for the Allegretto Cabernet Sauvignon comes from the Willow Creek sub-appellation in Paso Robles. This is one of the most coveted areas in the United States for growing ultra-premium Cabernet Sauvignon. The grapes are destemmed and then fermented in small open-top containers. After the fermentation is complete, the wine is aged in specially designed French oak barrels that are made only for Allegretto.

AWARDS & DISTINCTIONS
Gold Medal – San Francisco International Wine Competition

TECHNICAL DATA

APPELLATION: Willow Creek District
COMPOSITION: 100% Cabernet Sauvignon
MATURATION: Aged 30 months in 60 percent new French oak and 40 percent neutral French oak.
CELLARING: The remarkable wine drinks well now, and will continue to drink well for another 10 to 15 years.

LEARN MORE

Visit our website by scanning the image on left.

Special occasions at the resort are commemorated in the French-inspired Abbey, tucked along the cloistered courtyard that is reminiscent of a small European village.

Douglas' keen eye extends to the gardens and grounds as well. "Every varietal of plant and tree is chosen for its area because the land has a particular resonance and desires for that varietal to be planted there," says Douglas. "It's not simply my desire, or random. The land itself is completely involved in the decision of what is planted where."

The 20-acre resort is surrounded by vineyards and dotted with native oaks, redwoods, cedars, and liquid ambers. The fruit orchard is lush with pomegranates, Meyer lemons, Mission figs, and olives.

Planted on raised wooden beds, the chef's garden is a symphony of fragrant herbs and seasonal vegetables. The bounty is skillfully incorporated with the locally farmed and foraged delights served at the resort's Cello Ristorante & Bar.

When Ayres first came to Paso Robles, he was taken by its pastoral beauty and warmth of the locals. It wasn't long before he acquired a 17-acre vineyard planted to premium Cabernet Sauvignon in Paso Robles' famed Willow Creek District and named the vineyard to honor the district.

TOP: The Tannat Vineyard on the east side of the resort.

BELOW: The 12,000-square-foot Piazza del Magica sits at the heart of the Allegretto Vineyard Resort.
Photographs courtesy of Allegretto Vineyard Resort

Willow Creek Vineyard's 90-acre hillside is perched at an elevation of 1,750 feet surrounded by oaks, redwoods, sequoias, and walnut trees. Sustainable farming is practiced in the 20-acre vineyard planted in clay loam soils topped with calcareous rock. Certain principles of organic and biodynamic farming are practiced, incorporating biodynamic applications of special homeopathic teas. An additional 20-acre pasture was added to the Allegretto portfolio on the east side in the Estrella District.

Douglas established Allegretto wines in 2013. While searching for the perfect name for the winery and resort, he decided on Allegretto, a musical term that means to play with a cheerful tempo. It also describes a life lived joyfully, in harmony and with intention.

Integral to all operations of the resort, Douglas is also involved with all aspects of the winery including overseeing the production of wine barrels, applying his knowledge of numerology to this craft. Winemaking is done by the careful hands of award-winning winemaker Alan Kinne.

The annual case production is a mere 2,000 cases of artisanal wines that are age-worthy, reflecting Paso's bright fruit with a layer of sophistication. The Duetto blend is a co-fermentation of Viognier and Vermentino; the jasmine-scented Viognier is brightened with subtle notes of honeysuckle.

TOP LEFT: The centerpiece of Allegretto's lobby is the fiber-optic chandelier reminiscent of the shape of the torus, that hangs above the central staircase.

TOP RIGHT: The passageways of Allegretto are designed to delight the senses as guests move about the resort, encouraging them to find peace during their stay.

ABOVE: The beating heart of Allegretto is the The Womb Creation Fountain which lies in the center of the resort and The Piazza del Magica.
Photographs courtesy of Allegretto Vineyard Resort

TANNAT

GOURMET PAIRINGS

Pair with pan-seared Australian rack of lamb with Allegretto pomegranate, brown-butter-roasted sweet potatoes, oak-grilled chard, and broccoli.

TASTING NOTES

The wine is medium bodied with the classic notes of Tannat. Cinnamon and anise, followed by hints of red cherries are also present. It's rich yet supple, with a lingering finish.

WINEMAKER'S INSIGHT

Allegretto is one of the few wineries in California that specializes in Tannat. The variety originates in southwestern France and has found a real home here in Paso Robles. The grapes are grown at the Allegretto Resort Vineyard. After careful hand-harvesting, the grapes are destemmed and fermented in small open-top containers. After the fermentation is complete, the grapes are pressed into a combination of American and French oak and aged for nearly two years.

AWARDS & DISTINCTIONS

Double Gold – San Francisco Chronicle Wine Competition
Double Gold – San Francisco International Wine Competition

TECHNICAL DATA

APPELLATION: Paso Robles
COMPOSITION: 100% Tannat
MATURATION: Aged 22 Months in 20 percent new American oak and 80 percent in neutral French oak.
CELLARING: This Tannat can be enjoyed now, yet will continue to age beautifully for an additional five to ten years.

ORDER OUR WINE

Buy our wines by scanning the image on left.

DUETTO

GOURMET PAIRINGS
Pair with butterleaf seafood salad with grilled octopus, whole prawns, and house-made Romanesco sauce.

TASTING NOTES
Co-fermenting Viognier and Vermentino produces balanced acidity with aromas of cardamom and orange blossom. This light-bodied wine is rounded out with notes of pineapple and crisp apple.

WINEMAKER'S INSIGHT
All of the grapes for this unique white wine are grown at the Allegretto Resort Vineyard. The Viognier and Vermentino are harvested together. After chilling the grapes overnight, they are gently pressed to extract the highest quality juice. The clean, settled juice is fermented in neutral oak barrels for nearly two years before bottling.

AWARDS & DISTINCTIONS
93 points – *Wine Enthusiast*
Gold Medal – San Francisco Chronicle Wine Competition

TECHNICAL DATA

APPELLATION: Paso Robles
COMPOSITION: 50% Viognier, 50% Vermentino
MATURATION: Aged 16 months in neutral French oak.
CELLARING: This wine is excellent now and will continue to age beautifully for the next two to four years.

LEARN MORE

Learn about our wine club and special offers to our members by scanning the image on the left.

In the red portfolio, Allegretto's double gold Tannat is a robust wine with classic notes of cinnamon and cherries; and the Malbec is redolent with blackberry and plum aromas; and the opulent Cabernet Sauvignon shows a velvety finish.

The contemporary Allegretto wine tasting room opens up to the 12,000 square-foot Piazza del Magica, anchored by six 100-year-old olive trees and reminiscent of Florence's famous palazzos and cloisters of the Benedictine monasteries.

The resort is a soul-sustaining sanctuary–a world unto itself where guests can engage in exceptional experiences, tour the halls' art and antiques, find quiet in the Abbey, rejuvenate with yoga, or lounge with a glass of Allegretto wine in the Piazza del Magica.

TOP: Winemaker Alan Kinne, and Proprietor Douglas Ayres barrel sampling the newest vintage.
Photograph by Linden Clover

MIDDLE: Harvest is a special time at Allegretto Vineyard resort each fall.
Photograph by Oak & Barrel Photography + Films

RIGHT: Proprietor Douglas Ayres sampling the estate Cabernet Sauvgnon before harvest.
Photograph by Oak & Barrel Photography + Films

TOP: Cabernet Sauvignon vines on the Willow Creek Vineyard.
Photograph by Sarah Kathleen Photography

LEFT: Proprietor Douglas Ayres during harvest of our Cabernet Sauvignon grapes in the Willow Creek Vineyard.
Photograph by Sarah Kathleen Photography

ABOVE: Allegretto Wines' tasting flight ready for guests.
Photograph by Linden Clover

MALBEC

GOURMET PAIRINGS

Pair with fresh pasta, arugula pesto, Malbec-braised portobello mushroom, heirloom tomato, brûléed Brie, and balsamic pearls.

TASTING NOTES

Reminiscent of harvest time in the vineyard, this medium bodied wine has aromas of ripe blackberries and notes of leather and tart currants

WINEMAKER'S INSIGHT

The Malbec grapes are grown near the resort in Paso Robles. Although Malbec is not an overly common varietal in Paso Robles, proprietor Douglas Ayres found that the Allegretto Resort property took naturally to the vines and produced complex fruit. After the grapes are harvested and destemmed, they are then set to ferment in small open-top containers. The pressed, fermented juice is moved to a combination of American oak and neutral French oak barrels to age for three years.

TECHNICAL DATA

APPELLATION: Paso Robles

COMPOSITION: 100% Malbec

MATURATION: Aged 36 months in 50 percent new American oak and 50 percent neutral French oak.

CELLARING: This Malbec can be enjoyed now, yet will continue to age beautifully for an additional five to 10 years.

ORDER OUR WINE

Buy our wines by scanning the image on left.

Brecon Estate   PASO ROBLES

Owner and winemaker Damian Grindley's passion for wine and wanderlust has taken him from England and South Wales to Australia and now Paso Robles. Paying homage to his Gaelic heritage, Grindley founded Brecon Estate (it's both a cathedral town and a National Park in South Wales) in 2012 with his wife, Amanda, and partners Simon and Anna Hackett.

Looking back it all makes sense to the proud Welshman. He had a vegetable patch as a teenager and sold organic produce on the pavement. This led to his first degree in horticulture-viticulture while a casual job at a liquor wholesaler honed his palate and led to a successful career in the U.K. wine industry. Grindley later pursued his postgraduate qualification in enology at Australia's prestigious University of Adelaide.

Located in Paso Robles' westside Adelaida District, Brecon produces a range of varietals from Albariño to Zinfandel with Rhône and Bordeaux blends in between. The ranch was once owned by Mennonites and by Jesse James' uncle, providing a hangout for the young outlaw. The property, noted for calcareous soils, is recognized for one of the earliest plantings of Bordeaux varietals, most of which survive to this day and are the backbone of Brecon wines.

FACING PAGE: The patio at Brecon Estate offers an informal and restful tasting experience of our signature wines.

ABOVE: Damian, Amanda, and Merran Grindley tend to the Brecon Estate Old Vine Cabernet Sauvignon Vineyard. *Photograph by Chris Leshinsky*

Enjoy a more formal tasting in the contemporary indoor lounge or relax on the alfresco terrace, shaded by heritage oaks where you can mosey up to the tasting bar with your muddy boots and friendly hounds and savor Brecon's hand-crafted wines. Brecon is open daily and tours are by appointment.

BrochelleVineyards PASO ROBLES

The founders of Brochelle Vineyards are grateful for the opportunity to express their artistic voices by creating wines that end up playing a part in some of life's most simple pleasures. Wine is used as a catalyst to commemorate joyous occasions and honor relationships and life's milestones, and creating something that has been used to share in these most intimate of times has truly been one of the greatest privileges of their vocation. Owner and operators, and husband-and-wife team, Brock and Michelle Waterman don't take this responsibility lightly and have used it as a motivating force behind their small-but-mighty winery since establishing in 1998. When Brock and Michelle's relationship began in the late 1990s, they shared one memorable bottle of Paso Robles Zinfandel and it changed the course of their lives forever. They both fell in love with the rolling hills on the Westside of Paso Robles and each other, and that is where their story began.

Located on 20 acres on a steep Westside hilltop in Paso Robles, Brochelle Vineyards uses a pure, no-fuss approach to winemaking. The grapes are always encouraged to speak for themselves and treated with the greatest of care—this way, they'll quietly but surely reveal where they came from. The team uses Old World farming and winemaking techniques, and the boutique vineyard is purposely geared to produce small yields of intense, flavorful fruit. With minimal intervention during the winemaking process, the grapes truly reveal themselves in the glass. Estate-grown varieties include Zinfandel, Grenache, Syrah, Petite Sirah, Mourvèdre, and Alicante Bouschet.

FACING PAGE: Our Estate vineyard is set on steep hillsides on the westside of Paso Robles. Our vines are head-pruned and dry-farmed for premium quality.
Photograph by Peter Schroeder

TOP: The Waterman family: Bryson, Brock, Michelle, and Braden
Photograph by Jill Hewston

ESTATE PETITE SIRAH

GOURMET PAIRINGS

This extremely lush and full-bodied wine is a perfect marriage with red meat and game as well as hearty stews and winter broths. Pair with cassoulet, coq au vin, short ribs, and duck entrées. For dessert, it is complementary with dark chocolate mousse and anything not overly sweet, as the wine provides a deep richness all on its own.

TASTING NOTES

Sit down for this one, as our Petite Sirah is an undeniably massive wine. Inky dark purple, viscous, and lush, the wine will leave you simply in awe. It's round and full yet maintains a bright acidity that keeps it from being heavy. The estate premium fruit produces this beauty of a wine, as it is highly fragranced with an essence of dried rose petal and dark berries. Layered between dark berry flavors, melted chocolate and creamy mocha cross your palate, complemented by tannins that are fully developed.

WINEMAKER'S INSIGHT

A very limited amount of Petite Sirah, a mere 1,000 vines, is grown on the steeply sloped hillside vineyard in the Adelaida District of Paso Robles. The hot days and much cooler nights are the prime growing area for this late-ripening, thin-skinned grape. At harvest, these grapes are so intense they stain hands, bins, and equipment immediately upon crush. The fruit is dry-farmed, head-trained, and night-hand harvested. The wine is neither fined nor filtered before bottling.

AWARDS & DISTINCTIONS

89 points – *Wine Enthusiast*

Silver Medal – *Central Coast Wine Competition*

TECHNICAL DATA

APPELLATION: Paso Robles, Adelaida District

COMPOSITION: 100% Petite Sirah

MATURATION: Aged for 18 months in 80 percent French and 20 percent American oak barrels.

CELLARING: Drinkable in its youth, the wine has a profound tannin structure that allows graceful aging for 18-plus years.

LEARN MORE

Visit our website by scanning the image on left.

All the wines produced by Brochelle are personally hand-crafted by Brock himself. Total overall production has remained around 3,500 cases throughout the past several years in order to focus on producing nothing but premium wines. For Brock and Michelle, wine is their artistry and is crafted through an intensely intuitive process. Their attention to detail is apparent with every vintage, and you will discover robust flavors, velvety richness, and an undoubted elegance in each of their wines. You'll find something a little different about Brochelle's wines, something tangible. They feel it's because their passion for their craft shines through in every bottle—it's what they strive for.

Brock and Michelle have a drive for excellence and pursue it daily in everything they do. For elite access to Brochelle's wines, consider joining the Wine Club to become a part of their extended family. You'll obtain the opportunity to experience

TOP: Sunset in our estate vineyard on the westside of Paso Robles, Adelaida District AVA.

RIGHT: Refillable growler bottles are located inside our tasting lounge and are filled with either Zinfandel or Chardonnay from our tap system. Guests are encouraged to return the bottles for refills at a discount. Perfect for parties, camping, or the beach!
Photographs by Michelle Waterman

wines allocated exclusively for the Wine Club and attend members-only events. Members receive two shipments per year and include the Reserve wines and Club-Only releases. Options for Membership include three, six, or 12 bottle shipments and receive 10, 15, or 20 percent off the retail prices, respectively. They also cater to the varietal-specific enthusiast by offering Zinfandel Only and Cabernet Only Club Memberships.

Brochelle's tasting room is beautifully decorated, cozy and welcoming, and an ideal coastal getaway for the day. Conveniently located in an urban setting, it is easy to get to when traveling in Paso Robles as it is right off Highway 46 East, close to downtown. Open daily from 11 am -5 pm, it is the recommended stop when wine tasting in the area.

TOP & MIDDLE: Our tasting lounge is conveniently located close to town in an urban setting. It is styled to look and feel like a chic living room, and patrons love the warm and comfy vibe we've created for them to sit and stay awhile while enjoying our wines.

LEFT: Our flagship wine is our iconic Zinfandel which is head-pruned and dry-farmed to achieve the ultimate in lush flavors and mouthfeel.
Photographs by Michelle Waterman

ESTATE ZINFANDEL

GOURMET PAIRINGS

With a subtle spicy sweetness, our Zinfandel is a perfect accompaniment for steaks, burgers, grilled veggies, or with zesty tomato-based pasta dishes. It pairs beautifully with an assortment of cheeses and cured or smoked meats.

TASTING NOTES

The 18th vintage of our renowned Zinfandel is fresh and vibrant in its youth and crafted to maintain luster into the cellar, as well. Bursting with fragrant berry fruits combined with a slight, delicate spice and a rich essence of cocoa, this opulent wine is brimming with fruit up front, and then softly textured throughout, making it luxurious and decadent.

WINEMAKER'S INSIGHT

The wine is sourced from our estate vineyard, planted in 1997 on a thoughtfully selected 20-acre plot on Paso Robles' westside. The Zinfandel vines are dry-farmed and head-trained, and the grapes are night-hand harvested. It is neither fined nor filtered before bottling. Out of all the wines from the cellar, this is our customers' top preferred entertaining wine, as it is always a crowd favorite. The Zinfandel is available in traditional 750-ml wine bottles and 32- or 64-ounce growler bottles—perfect for sharing with friends.

TECHNICAL DATA

APPELLATION: Paso Robles, Adelaida District
COMPOSITION: 100% Zinfandel
MATURATION: Aged for 14 months in 80 percent French and 20 percent American oak barrels.
CELLARING: Is vibrant and approachable now, but the precise balance of acidity and tannins enable for long-term aging for 15-plus years.

ORDER OUR WINE

Buy our wines by scanning the image on left.

CaliPaso Winery PASO ROBLES

Somewhere between California's two largest metropolitan areas lies a quiet getaway, nestled in the rolling hills of Paso Robles. CaliPaso is a luxurious inn and winery set on the Central Coast between Los Angeles and San Francisco and is the perfect example of why the region is famous for its wine and beauty.

Long interested in the wine business, in 2012, Mr. Wu was originally searching for opportunities in the Napa Valley area, until he had a chance to visit the CaliPaso property in the Estrella region of Paso Robles. For Mr. Wu and his family, it was love at first sight, and they acquired the property soon after. Still today, CaliPaso Winery is a family-owned winery that takes great pride in showing off the hospitality of the area as well as its wines.

CaliPaso's estate vineyards were originally planted in 1981. The majority of the vineyard is currently producing three of the eight major Italian varietals: Sangiovese, Primitivo, and Nebbiolo. However, work has already begun on replacing those vines with Cabernet Sauvignon, which the winery has already had immense success in growing on a small plot directly behind the inn. In addition to estate-grown offerings, they produce Cuvée Blanc which is a white Rhône blend, Chardonnay, Zinfandel, Tempranillo, and Pinot Noir.

The grape-growing climate in Paso Robles is ideal for the production of award-winning premium wines. A long growing season of warm days and cool evenings gives rise to vibrantly ripened fruit with dynamic flavor profiles that make some of the world's finest wines. The winery is currently distributing to 17 states and plans to increase that number and increase sustainable

FACING PAGE: A romantic wedding venue in Paso Robles, CaliPaso Winery and Villa beautifully mixes the appeal of a charming French winery with hues of California to create the ultimate setting for all types of events. The architectural beauty offers a picturesque location that makes for unique and lovely wedding photos.

ABOVE: Twelve unique varieties of wines, produced by CaliPaso, can be enjoyed at our winery.
Photographs by Brandon Stier

CALIPASO CHARDONNAY

GOURMET PAIRINGS
The Chardonnay pairs well with most dishes but is best enjoyed with a simple grilled fish.

TASTING NOTES
CaliPaso Chardonnay is a drink-all-day Chardonnay. Fresh pear, citrus notes, and soft acidity allow for this wine to be readily enjoyed for any occasion.

WINEMAKER'S INSIGHT
The CaliPaso Chardonnay is made in a classic Old World style. The grapes are hand-harvested from local Paso Robles vineyards and then whole-cluster pressed to retain the maximum varietal characteristics. After cold settling, the clean juice is racked into a combination of neutral French oak barrels and stainless steel and cool fermented—less than 60 degrees—to keep the beautiful fruitiness. After fermentation, the wine is aged sur lies (on the yeast) for seven months to add to its complexity.

AWARDS & DISTINCTIONS
Silver Medal – Los Angeles International Wine Competition
Gold Medal – Rodeo Houston International Wine Competition

TECHNICAL DATA

APPELLATION: Paso Robles
COMPOSITION: 100% Chardonnay
MATURATION: Aged for seven months in a combination of 85 percent neutral French oak and 15 percent stainless steel tanks.
CELLARING: Delicious now, but will cellar beautifully for three years.

Learn more about CaliPaso wines

TOP LEFT: CaliPaso Vineyard in summer

TOP RIGHT: The natural, curved hill is perfect for looking at the outdoor stage at CaliPaso winery.

BELOW LEFT: Grapes being sorted during the fall harvest.

BELOW RIGHT: A winery worker shoveling out fermented grapes from the wine storage is just one of the steps in crafting a great wine.
Photographs by Brandon Stier

production over the next few years. While looking to grow, they remain committed to taking their time to develop relationships with growers, distributors and customers. Producing wines that exemplify their commitment to everyone involved is their primary goal.

Alan Kinne, CaliPaso's Director of Winemaking, has been recognized as one of the leaders in the wine industry for more than 30 years. His multifaceted career has crisscrossed the country's wine regions, all the while gaining knowledge and prestige. Alan started his career in Michigan after graduating from the University of Michigan, and managed wineries and made wine in Virginia. He later went on to do the same on Long Island before returning to Virginia to start his award-winning consulting service. During the decade when he was exclusively a consultant, Alan received numerous accolades and recognition. One of his proudest achievements is introducing several new varieties of grapes to the United States. These include Albariño, Graciano, Petit Manseng, and a new selection of Tempranillo. He

then spent nearly 10 years as a winemaker in Paso Robles before working in the Willamette Valley of Oregon and again in Virginia. During this time, he began consulting for CaliPaso before being named the Director of Winemaking in 2013. Assistant winemaker Enrique Torres works side by side with Alan (they have worked together for over 15 years), and together they operate under the simple philosophy that great wines are a natural art form where the hand of man is lightly placed to direct the results.

As the early summer morning mist was beginning to clear in 2013, Jaime Glenn sat in the courtyard and listened as Mr. Wu shared his vision for the winery. Having worked in the wine industry for almost two decades, Jaime knew something special when she saw it. She joined the company as Chief Operating Officer and brought a unique blend of talents and values to CaliPaso Winery

TOP: Visitors and locals enjoy tasting our 12 wines during sports night at our tasting room.

RIGHT: Another popular activity at our tasting room are art classes where wine and fun are in abundance..
Photographs by Brandon Stier

CALIPASO ESTATE CABERNET

GOURMET PAIRINGS
Balanced acidity and smooth tannins give this wine a structure that pairs well with a variety of foods, including filet mignon or summer barbecue favorites such as smoked ribs and tri-tip.

TASTING NOTES
The Calipaso Estate Cabernet is a supple yet substantial wine.

WINEMAKER'S INSIGHT
The CaliPaso Estate Cabernet Sauvignon is produced from one of the oldest plantings of the variety in Paso Robles. The grapes are sourced from the CaliPaso estate's nearly 40-year-old vines that produce small yields of flavorful fruit. All of the hand-picked grapes are gently destemmed and fermented in stainless steel tanks. For extraction, the tanks are pumped over twice daily and pressed off when dry.

AWARDS & DISTINCTIONS
Silver Medal – Los Angeles International Wine Competition
Silver Medal – San Francisco Chronicle Wine Competition

TECHNICAL DATA

APPELLATION: Paso Robles
COMPOSITION: 100% Estate Cabernet Sauvignon
MATURATION: The new wine is aged for approximately 18 months in a combination of new and used French oak barrels.
CELLARING: This wine will age gracefully up to 10 years.

ORDER OUR WINE

Visit our wine store by scanning the image to left

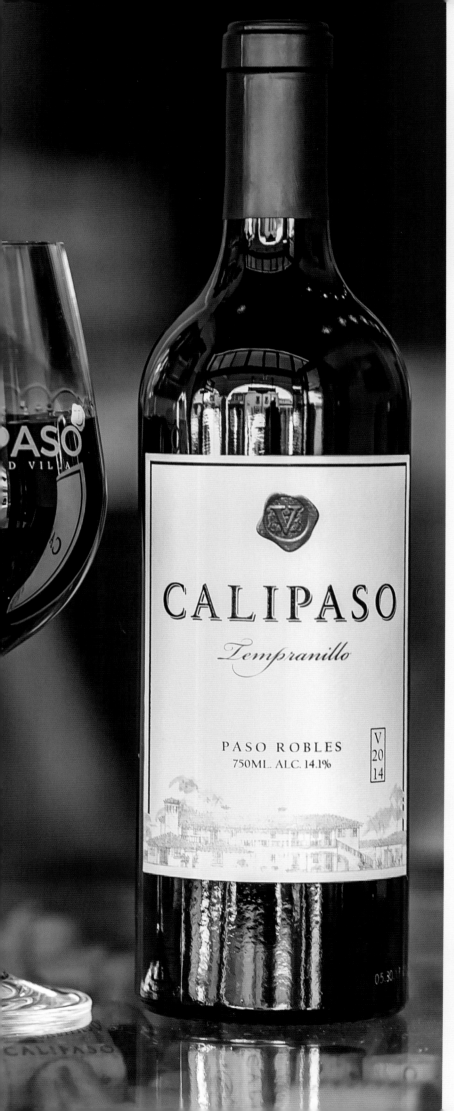

CALIPASO TEMPRANILLO

GOURMET PAIRINGS

This is such a versatile wine that pairs well with everything from rib-eye to chile rellenos.

TASTING NOTES

CaliPaso Tempranillo is loaded with flavors of blueberries, currants, and dark chocolate. The wine has a velvety mouthfeel with a lingering finish that is warm and fulfilling.

WINEMAKER'S INSIGHT

The CaliPaso Tempranillo is sourced from grapes that came from vines that the winemaker, Alan Kinne, brought over from Spain more than 20 years ago. He has several vineyards of Tempranillo planted in the Paso Robles appellation and every year chooses his favorite grapes from the vintage. The grapes are destemmed and fermented using a combination of punch downs and pump-overs to gain maximum extraction

AWARDS & DISTINCTIONS

Gold, Class Champion – Rodeo Houston International Wine Competition
Double Gold – San Francisco Chronicle Wine Competition

TECHNICAL DATA

APPELLATION: Paso Robles
COMPOSITION: 100% Tempranillo
MATURATION: The finished wine is aged for over 24 months in a combination of American and French oak (which is traditional in Spain) with 25 percent new.
CELLARING: Cellar now for up to 10 years.

LEARN MORE

Learn more CaliPaso wines

and Villa. Her experience, dedication to the industry as a whole, and love for CaliPaso wines has helped CaliPaso get to where it is today. Her involvement in the community, hosting, and sponsoring fundraisers throughout the years has put CaliPaso on the map as one of the top venue destinations for weddings and special events on the Central Coast, hosting 30 weddings in 2018. In 2017, the establishment opened an offsite tasting room in downtown Paso Robles to better accommodate and serve the increasing visitors to CaliPaso Winery and Villa.

Known for its warm, personal service, the inn features seven guestrooms and suites, all which offer elegant decor that combines luxury and comfort. Features include fireplaces, private balconies, and patios overlooking the vineyards and surrounding countryside. The rooms are affectionately named after wines and spirits, such as the Grappa, Merlot, and Cabernet Suites. Among the accommodations is the Winemaker's Cottage. It's an exclusive 1,500-square-foot, two-room suite that is appointed with an international look and Italian-inspired touches. Its location offers sweeping panoramic views of the Paso Robles countryside and surrounding vineyards, and

TOP: A night view of the beautiful and inviting setting at the CaliPaso Winery and Villas.

MIDDLE: A view of the Winemaker Resident Room.

RIGHT: CaliPaso Winery and Villa Room view
Photograph s by Brandon Stier

includes a resplendent living room with fine imported European furniture and a large fireplace. The dining room comfortably seats ten and is supported by a beautiful kitchen to enhance any private entertaining. Two luxurious king bed guestrooms connect the grand living area, and a private patio enhances a stay here. Unique custom finishing touches are everywhere. This cottage is ideal for a honeymoon, romantic vacation, or as a corporate master suite.

Peaceful, stunning, and beautifully placed in the coastal region, CaliPaso is a getaway for wine lovers. Tuscan-inspired, the entire venue has an Old World ambiance that makes you feel like you're in Italy—the ideal setting to exchange vows. The winery participates in annual events and festivals, so make sure to check the website for the most up-to-date information.

TOP: A magical view of CaliPaso Winery and Villa under the stars.

RIGHT: Our executive chef is shown preparing dishes during one of many events and CaliPaso Winery.
Photographs by Brandon Stier

THREE HOUNDS PINOT NOIR

GOURMET PAIRINGS
Perfect pairings for this bold Pinot Noir would be charcuterie or any roasted meats.

TASTING NOTES
The Three Hounds Pinot Noir is the definition of accessible sophistication. It is confident and elegant with ample flavors of plum and black cherries. This is an amazing Pinot Noir for the price.

WINEMAKER'S INSIGHT
CaliPaso Three Hounds Pinot Noir is one of our reserve wines. Made from grapes from one of the finest vineyards in the Santa Maria Valley, this wine was whole-cluster, barrel fermented with gentle punch downs three times a day. After fermentation, the wine was aged in the same combination of new and used French oak barrels for an additional nine months prior to bottling. The wine is classic Burgundian in style with a remarkable finesse.

TECHNICAL DATA

APPELLATION: Santa Maria Valley
COMPOSITION: 100% Pinot Noir
MATURATION: Aged for nine months in a combination of 80 percent neutral French oak and 20 percent new French oak.
CELLARING: This wine will age gracefully up to 10 years.

ORDER OUR WINE

Visit our wine store by scanning the image to left

Derby Wine Estates PASO ROBLES

Ray and Pam Derby, founders of their eponymous winery, have created an ambitious wine estate. Three vineyards in three Paso Robles growing regions planted to 25 different wine grapes, ranging from Bordeaux and Rhône to Burgundian and Spanish varieties, cause the affable Ray Derby to remark that their varieties planted range "from Albariño to Zinfandel."

Ray, a former manufacturer of automobile parts in Southern California and his wife, Pam, moved to the coastal hamlet of Cambria along the Central Coast in the 1990s. With the intention of retiring, they purchased their San Simeon ranch in a cool wind-swept region near the famed Hearst Castle. They named it Derbyshire.

The ocean-view, hilltop property where the Derbys planted Pinot Noir and Pinot Gris vineyards was part of the Hearst Ranch that William Randolph Hearst's father, Senator George Hearst, purchased from Ira Van Gordon and later sold in the late 1930s to a cattleman from Arroyo Grande. After a couple of different owners, the Derbys acquired the rugged terrain of 632 acres in 1998. San Simeon itself is not an AVA (American Viticultural Area) but rather lies adjacent to the Paso Robles AVA.

The wind-swept Derbyshire vineyard is the closest commercial vineyard to the Pacific Ocean and comes with its own set of challenges such as fierce winds that can damage the fruit. The Derbys consulted with a number of vineyard experts but most of them were dubious. The concern was about fruit ripening.

FACING PAGE: The entrance to the Derby Wine Estates' winery is a restored 1922 almond processing plant.
Photograph by Matthew Anderson

TOP LEFT: Derby Wine Estates offers wines from three different vineyards located in three unique growing regions of San Luis Obispo County.
Photograph by Brandon Stier, Oak & Barrel Photography

TOP RIGHT: Ray and Pam Derby, the proud proprietors of Derby Wine Estates.
Photograph by Chris Leschinsky

SAN LUIS OBSIPO COUNTY

'1510' WHITE RHONE BLEND

GOURMET PAIRINGS
Pair with pan-seared scallops on angel hair pasta with a basil, parsley, and lemon butter sauce.

TASTING NOTES
A blend of five White Rhône grapes grown at the Derby Vineyard, this wine displays aromas of honeydew, nectarine, and apricot with additional flavors of granite and homemade buttered popcorn.

WINEMAKER'S INSIGHT
Grapes were hand-harvested throughout the month of September at night and delivered to the winery by 7 a.m. to preserve acidity and freshness. Individual lots were fermented and aged in a combination of stainless steel, new Acacia barrels, and amphora, and bottled within six months of harvest.

AWARDS & DISTINCTIONS
90 points – Bev X
Editors' Choice – *Wine Enthusiast*

TECHNICAL DATA

APPELLATION: Paso Robles, Templeton Gap District
COMPOSITION: 34% Viognier, 20% Marsanne, 18% Picpoul Blanc, 18% Roussanne, 9% Grenache Blanc
MATURATION: The 1510 White Rhône Blend is a combination of five Rhone varieties, each with its own protocol, and thus no single maturation protocol.
CELLARING: Delicious now, but will cellar beautifully for three years.

LEARN MORE

Learn more about Derby Wine Estates by scanning image on the left

TOP: The Derbyshire Vineyard, located a mere one mile from the Pacific Ocean, is the source of the Derby's Burgundian varieties.
Photograph by Chris Leschinsky

BELOW: The Derby Winery building was built in 1922 and "illuminated to draw the admiration of the travelers along both the State Highway and the railroad."
Photograph by Matthew Anderson

Ray, however, was intrigued by the hardships of this region and took a leap of faith on the San Simeon ranch which was nothing more than grazing land at the time.

Challenges notwithstanding, Ray is proud of the risk he's taken. The result is a small-lot production of distinctive Pinot Noir, Pinot Gris, Chardonnay and cool climate Syrah from this extreme region.

From this cool region, the Derbys expanded their plantings to Paso Robles proper. On the east side, they acquired the 278-acre Laura's Vineyard in the Estrella District that is planted to Bordeaux varieties. The vineyard was once part of the Estrella River Winery, with its historical roots spanning over three decades.

On the west side of Paso Robles, they added the 129-acre property, in the cool Templeton Gap region, re-naming it Derby Vineyard. The vineyard was already planted to 35 acres of Rhône varieties, to which Spanish and Bordeaux varieties were added.

This estate also serves as the Derbys' scenic residence perched high above the vineyards.

Touring the winery itself with Ray is like a walk back in time. The building, once an almond warehouse and processing plant, was forced to shut down in the 1930s as almond productivity declined. The building went through a few owners and sat abandoned. It was ready to be demolished, when the Derbys stepped in. They purchased it in 2010 and converted it into a state-of-the art winery and contemporary tasting room whose hallways are lined with vintage photos and memorabilia from the building's historic past.

When the Derbys embarked on vineyard planting, the intention was to sell fruit. Over the years, the family has built up a reputation so that 95 percent of their grapes are purchased by noted California wineries. In 2005, though, they decided to launch their own label. Currently a small annual production of 3,000 cases is made with fruit sourced from some 20 hand-selected acres, allowing visitors to experience the full spectrum of the Derby Collection–from refreshing rosé and white wines to lush reds. Among them, the red and white Project España wines –the white, a refreshing Albariño driven blended with Grenache Blanc and the red, a bold Tempranillo blended with Graciano,

TOP: Ray and Pam Derby are justifiably proud of the 20 different grape varieties grown on their Paso Robles' Templeton Gap District vineyard.

BELOW: The history of the Derby Templeton Gap District Vineyard dates back to the early Templeton settlers.
Photographs by Chris Leschinsky

IMPLICO

GOURMET PAIRINGS

Serve this wine with a filet wrapped with thick-cut bacon and cooked medium rare. Add an Implico-based peppercorn sauce.

TASTING NOTES

As its name suggests, this wine is an "intimate connection" of four Bordeaux varieties: Cabernet Sauvignon, Cabernet Franc, Malbec, and Merlot. It displays aromas of dark fruits, graphite, anise, and cedar with additional flavors of raspberry, cassis, and tobacco.

WINEMAKER'S INSIGHT

Hand-harvested during the months of September and October, the grapes are from individual lots that were processed and aged separately prior to blending. After blending, this wine was given additional aging prior to bottling.

AWARDS & DISTINCTIONS

Best of Class – *San Francisco Chronicle*
Silver Medal – Orange County Fair

TECHNICAL DATA

APPELLATION: Paso Robles
COMPOSITION: 33% Cabernet Franc, 27% Malbec, 24% Cabernet Sauvignon, 15% Merlot
MATURATION: Aged for 32 months in 15 percent new French oak and 85 percent neutral French oak barrels.
CELLARING: Ready to drink upon release but can be cellared for up to 15 years.

ORDER OUR WINE

Visit our wine store by scanning the image to left

DERBYSHIRE VINEYARD PINOT NOIR

GOURMET PAIRINGS

Pair with oven-baked pork roulade with garlic rosemary rub, stuffed with mushrooms and shallots sautéed in Pinot Noir. Serve with brown sugar and butter-glazed baby carrots.

TASTING NOTES

The wine is vibrant magenta in color with beautiful notes of fresh cherry, cranberry, and raspberry.

WINEMAKER'S INSIGHT

The Pinot Noir fruit was hand-harvested at 25.2 Brix from the Derbyshire Vineyard. It was destemmed at the winery and cold soaked at 45 degrees for two days in a temperature-controlled tank and then inoculated and fermented. Once dry, the lot was gently pressed in a basket press, transferred to barrels, inoculated with ML culture, and aged for 10 months.

AWARDS & DISTINCTIONS

93 points – *Wine Enthusiast*
Silver Medal – *San Francisco Chronicle*

TECHNICAL DATA

APPELLATION: San Simeon, San Luis Obispo County
COMPOSITION: 100% Pinot Noir
MATURATION: Aged 10 months in French Oak, 33 percent new.
CELLARING: Enjoy now and anytime within the next five years.

LEARN MORE

Learn more about Derby Wine Estates by scanning image on the left

Grenache and Carignane. The Fifteen10 series highlight both red and white Rhône blends and the Implico, a complex Bordeaux style wine, is brilliantly blended with fruit from both east side and west side vineyards. The Maneater, a blend of Zinfandel and Petite Sirah, flexes its muscle with a layer of elegance.

Growing 25 different grape varieties is not only an advantage when it comes to offering unique blends, but it also gives Derby the opportunity to offer special and unique single varietal wines to a select clientele in limited quantities. These "Black Label" wines are made from a single grape varietal grown on a single Derby-owned vineyard, selected from the choicest barrel lots, and produced and bottled in extremely limited quantities.

A special reserve tasting of library wines is offered every Saturday afternoon in the exclusive Almond Room in the building's tower that offers a 360-degree view of Paso Robles.

The Derbys passion for hand-crafted and exceptional wines is present in each bottle that reflects the diverse spectrum of Paso Robles, from Burgundian and Spanish to Rhône and Bordeaux style wines.

TOP: The Derby Wine Estates Tasting Room harkens back to the Art Deco style of the 1920s.

MIDDLE: Wines are processed and aged under tightly controlled conditions in the winery.

RIGHT: Laura's Vineyard, in Paso Robles' Estrella District, is home to Derby's Bordeaux varieties.
Photographs by Matthew Anderson

Donati Family Vineyard TEMPLETON

Like most Italian immigrants, Albino Donati made his own wine for the family dinner table. The grandfather of Donati Family Vineyard founder Ron Donati came to America from Lucca, Italy, in 1907, and his belief in making quality products that were attainable to all inspired his grandson to establish the Templeton winery in 2007.

The family-run business—today, Ron's son Mark is owner and president—specializes in Bordeaux varietals, particularly Cabernet Sauvignon and Bordeaux blends. The versatility of the Paicines AVA allows the winery to also produce select amounts of Chardonnay, Pinot Blanc, Syrah, and Grenache. Located in the center of coastal California, a little over an hour from San Jose to the north and Monterey to the west, the Paicines AVA is in the heart of California's Greater Central Coast AVA and is open to the direct influence of the cool ocean air that flows to the San Joaquin Valley. In the afternoon, Paicines takes advantage of the slight cooling breeze that comes in off the Monterey Bay, while at night, Paicines is more protected from the evening fog than much of the surrounding area because of its open location.

The Donati Family Estate Vineyard site enjoys a variety of soils, from limestone to decomposed granite to clay loam. Hands-on, year-round vineyard management creates an environment where the grapes themselves can be left to ripen undisturbed—though active personnel regularly hand-tends the vines to check for any potential problems. A sustainable approach means that natural predators and reduced use of pesticides provide a clean, hospitable

FACING PAGE: The Donati Family Vineyard's winery and tasting room in Templeton.

ABOVE: Founders Ron and Alexis Donati enjoying life at the winery.
Photographs courtesy of Donati Family Vineyard, Inc.

CLARET

GOURMET PAIRINGS

Enjoy with smoked beef tenderloin, Yukon gold potato crisp, and shaved horseradish.

TASTING NOTES

"Claret" is the British term for a Bordeaux blended wine that dates back to the 13th century. The Claret tradition is kept alive by blending the five predominant Bordeaux varietals: Cabernet Sauvignon, Merlot, Malbec, Petit Verdot, and Cabernet Franc. This fruit-forward wine greets the drinker with blueberry cobbler and ripe plum, while Rainier cherries infuse with bright raspberries. Cranberry acidity lingers on the palate, with delicate mocha and hazelnut oak profiles.

WINEMAKER'S INSIGHT

Based on the vintage, the exact vineyard blocks and the varietal compositions change slightly, but the aim is always to produce the best possible blends from the estate vineyard as possible. The Cabernet Sauvignon and the Cabernet Franc berries are fermented in small open-top fermenters, while Malbec, Merlot, and Petit Verdot are fermented whole berry in static stainless tanks. All varietals and blocks are kept separate for over 14 months, until base blending begins. Once the base blend is made, the wine will age another eight to 10 months in oak.

AWARDS & DISTINCTIONS

91 Points – *Wine Enthusiast*

TECHNICAL DATA

APPELLATION: Paicines/Central Coast
COMPOSITION: 48% Cabernet Sauvignon, 32% Merlot, 10% Malbec, 6% Petit Verdot, 4% Cab Franc (depending on vintage)
MATURATION: Aged 24 to 26 months in Medium Plus oak barrels, which add toasted nuances of mocha and coffee to the blend. The wood is sourced from French, Eastern European, and American forests.
CELLARING: Drinkable on release, but has a cellaring potential of five-10 years.

LEARN MORE

Visit our website by scanning the image on left

environment for vine growth and fruit maturation, which the Donati family has found makes a significant difference in both the local environment and the ultimate grape and wine quality.

To create the intense color and flavor for which Donati wines are known, red grapes are destemmed and pumped directly into the fermentation tanks. Both static and open-top fermenters are used, and then the red wines are aged for 12 to 18 months in a combination of both French and American oak barrels from a select group of coopers. The red wines are bottled un-fined and unfiltered to preserve the natural flavors and aromas of the grape varietals. White wines benefit from a gentle whole cluster press, and then the juice is immediately transferred to stainless steel fermenters for a 24-hour cold settling. The white juice ferments for approximately 30 days at 55 degrees Fahrenheit until dry, yielding no residual sugar. Post primary fermentation, the whites are fined and filtered before being botted the following spring to preserve the aromatic qualities in each variety.

Head winemaker Briana Heywood joined the Donati Family Vineyard team in 2016, transitioning from a previous position as an enologist at neighboring J. Lohr Vineyards & Wines for seven years and internships at Eberle Winery and E. & J. Gallo Winery before that. In 2009, she earned her enology

TOP LEFT: Jorge hard at work during harvest–our favorite time of year–in the barrel room.

TOP RIGHT: Donati Family wines aging to perfection.

BELOW: Receiving high quality Central Coast fruit during harvest.
Photographs courtesy of Donati Family Vineyard, Inc.

and wine business degrees from California Polytechnic State University in San Luis Obispo. This experience in both small and large wineries has equipped Briana with a unique perspective on maintaining consistency of handcrafted premium wines in ever-increasing quantities.

Devoted fans and curious newcomers can taste the Donati Family Vineyard wines for themselves at the popular tasting room. The three-story building resembles a European chateau and is nestled in the hills of Templeton, offering picnic grounds and bocce ball courts. Appointments are encouraged, especially if you're bringing a crowd, but there will always be a warm welcome waiting for anyone who wants to try some of the best wine on California's central coast.

TOP LEFT: Winemaker for Donati Family Vineyard, Briana Heywood, inspecting the arriving fruit.

MIDDLE LEFT: Our customers enjoy both great wine and fun playing bocce at Donati.

BOTTOM LEFT: Owner Mark Donati, enjoying an evening of Donati wines with friends and family.

ABOVE: Owner, Mark Donati, is involved in all aspects of the winemaking process and can seen around the grounds daily.
Photographs courtesy of Donati Family Vineyard, Inc.

THE IMMIGRANT

GOURMET PAIRINGS

Pairs beautifully with bleu cheese crusted filet mignon, sautéed morels, and a side of double baked Yukon gold potatoes.
.

TASTING NOTES

Containing an average 36% new oak, this wine presents layers of complexity. Plum skin, Bing cherries, and boysenberry aromatics explode upon first inhalation. Defined, velvety tannins pair with mocha and raspberry jelly on the palate. Spiciness dances with nuances of white peppercorn, finishing in layers of crisp cherry tart dessert.

WINEMAKER'S INSIGHT

This wine contains 100 percent estate-grown Merlot—there are 35 acres of Merlot on the Donati Family Vineyard property. Whole berries undergo primary fermentation in stainless steel tanks and complete malolactic fermentation in oak barrels. From the various lots of clone and rootstock combinations, the best barrels are cherry-picked and reserved for the program.

AWARDS & DISTINCTIONS

90 Points – *Wine Enthusiast*

TECHNICAL DATA

APPELLATION: Paicines/Central Coast
COMPOSITION: 100% Merlot
MATURATION: Aged 30 to 32 months in oak barrels. The new wood is sourced from French, Russian, and American forests.
CELLARING: Enjoy on release, although it can be cellared up to 10-plus years.

ORDER OUR WINE

 Buy our wines by scanning the image on left.

Écluse Wines PASO ROBLES

Écluse Wines, created by Steve and Pam Lock, is a family-owned boutique winery located in Paso Robles. Their quest began in 1997 when they purchased 30 beautiful acres nestled in the scenic rolling hills on the Westside of Paso Robles in the desired Willow Creek AVA, which has become the foundation of their remarkable wines. Starting out as growers, Steve and Pam's philosophy has always been that great fruit makes great wine and they knew the soils of Lock Vineyard had the special terroir necessary to produce prized fruit. Since then, Écluse has become well known for hand-crafted, award-winning wines creating a small annual production of 2,500 to 3,000 cases.

Many ask about the name Écluse. The explanation is simple: écluse is French for the locks on the canals that gently carve their way through the remarkable French wine county. Since their last name is Lock, the name Écluse was born.

It seemed a natural progression for Steve to go from grower to winemaker. Knowing that the best wines begin in the vineyard, Steve spends a great deal of time there every year tending to the 25,000 vines that make up Lock Vineyard. The vines are pampered and then stressed when necessary to produce the highest quality of fruit possible given the nature of the terrain and microclimate. They use sustainable viticulture practices including water conservation and limited use of pesticides.

Since the release of their first vintage in 2002, Écluse has been honored in the noted *San Francisco Chronicle's* Wine Competition with numerous Best of Class awards, Double Golds and Gold Medals, along with the crowning achievement of winning the Sweepstakes Award for Best Red Wine for their 2008 Cabernet Sauvignon in the 2011 competition. To be honored by this competition, which

FACING PAGE: Beautiful fall colors in our estate Lock Vineyard at harvest
Photograph by Anthony La Duca

ABOVE LEFT: Winemaker and proprietor Steve Lock sampling one of our award-winning wines.
Photograph by Julia Perez

ABOVE RIGHT: Tasting through the wines while blending the 2016 vintage in preparation for bottling.
Photograph by Kelly Breitmeyer

is the largest gathering of American wines in the world, continues to validate their winemaking style of producing lush, silky, and perfectly balanced wines.

Écluse continues to enter their wines in this competition each year where every wine entered has garnered medals. They have also been honored over the years with high scores from noted critics and wine media—among them, Robert M. Parker, Jr., Jeb Dunnuck, *Wine Enthusiast*, the San Francisco International Wine Competition, Tanzer's International Wine Cellar, and Affairs of the Vine, to name a few.

The special terroir of Lock Vineyard produces extraordinary wines. These include their single varietal Cabernet Sauvignon, Syrah, Zinfandel, and Petite Sirah, along with a variety of blends: Ensemble, a Bordeaux-style blend; Rendition, a Rhône-style blend; Improv, an eclectic, improvisational red blend; and Insider, a limited production, hand-crafted blend inspired by their Insider Club. For

the white wine lovers, Écluse has two white wines: Prelude, a white Rhône-style blend and their popular Chardonnay.

Steve and Pam's passion for making exceptional small production wines with high quality fruit is evident in every bottle. Having control from the vineyard to the bottle ensures that Écluse will remain the wine that it is today. They invite you to discover the Écluse difference and join them for a memorable tasting experience to savor the wine that is truly Écluse.

TOP: Beautiful sunset at Lock Vineyard and the Écluse winery, located in the scenic rolling hills on the west side of Paso Robles in the Willow Creek AVA. *Photograph by Kelly Breitmeyer*

BELOW: The Écluse team is dedicated to producing hand-crafted, award-winning wines and offering a special atmosphere for their guests, treating them like family and friends, while providing an intimate Écluse experience. *Photograph by Salvatore La Casto*

ENSEMBLE

GOURMET PAIRINGS
This elegant Bordeaux-style blend pairs perfectly with grilled meats such as filet mignon and lamb.

TASTING NOTES
Ensemble is a Bordeaux-style blend of Cabernet Sauvignon, Merlot, Petit Verdot, Malbec, and Cabernet Franc. Incredibly rich in color, the wine has notes of sweet tobacco and vanilla that lead to blueberry pie on the nose. This full-bodied Bordeaux blend excites the palate with flavors of cranberry, bright red fruit, and dried cherries with good structure and perfect balance. Incredibly elegant, this wine is wonderful now but will continue to age beautifully.

WINEMAKER'S INSIGHT
When the grapes reach peak flavors, they are hand-harvested, sorted, and fermented in small open-top bins. The pressed juice is aged in oak barrels, hand-picked for each varietal.

AWARDS & DISTINCTIONS
Double Gold – San Francisco Chronicle Wine Competition
93 points – Robert Parker's Wine Advocate
92 points – *Wine Enthusiast*
90 points – Vinous

TECHNICAL DATA

APPELLATION: Paso Robles
COMPOSITION: 32% Petit Verdot, 26% Cabernet Sauvignon, 26% Merlot, 13% Cabernet Franc, and 3% Malbec
MATURATION: Aged for 18 months in 40 percent new oak—a combination of French, American, and Hungarian oak barrels.
CELLARING: Phenomenal now but can be cellared for seven to 10 years.

LEARN MORE

Visit our website by scanning the image on the left

J. Lohr Vineyards & Wines   PASO ROBLES

In the world of wine, where words like "pioneer" and "icon" are often overused, Jerry Lohr is the real deal. Perhaps more than any other vintner, Jerry has brought Central Coast wines to global prominence. For almost half a century, he has been a tireless advocate for the region he loves, championing innovation, sustainability, and a collaborative approach rooted in the belief that a rising tide lifts all boats.

In 2016, when Jerry became the third person in the history of *Wine Enthusiast Magazine's* Wine Star Awards to be honored as an American Wine Legend, publisher Adam Strum wrote, "What Robert Mondavi was to Napa Valley, Jerry Lohr is to the Central Coast, leading and elevating an entire viticultural region from Monterey to Paso Robles with perseverance, dedication, and a passion for quality."

Jerry was raised on a farm in South Dakota, where an understanding of how to coax the best crop from the earth was instilled at an early age. He applied these lessons when he planted his first vineyards in Monterey County in 1972. There, in the cool, windswept Arroyo Seco, J. Lohr quickly established a reputation for growing vibrant and beautiful, place-driven expressions of Chardonnay, Riesling, Valdiguié, and later, Pinot Noir. Dedicated to crafting wines that celebrated their vineyard roots, Jerry made the pioneering decision to bottle all J. Lohr wines with an appellation designation, bringing the name Monterey County into wine-drinking households across America.

FACING PAGE: The beautiful Hilltop Vineyard oak tree illuminated at night.

TOP: Jerry Lohr harvests some of the company's original Arroyo Seco vineyards circa 1974.
Photographs courtesy of J. Lohr Vineyards

In the late '70s, when Jerry turned his attention to making world-class Cabernet Sauvignon, he and his talented team had a clear vision.

J. LOHR
SEVEN OAKS CABERNET SAUVIGNON

GOURMET PAIRINGS

This wine's alluring fruit flavors pair deliciously with beef tenderloin topped with the savory and aromatic Seven Oaks Brown Sauce and seasonable vegetables, featured in Recipes from the J. Lohr Vineyard Table: Seven Oaks Cabernet Sauvignon booklet available in the Entertaining section of jlohr.com.

TASTING NOTES

From its dark color to its enticing aromas of black currant, blueberry, and cherry, this lush and inviting wine offers a beautiful snapshot of what makes Paso Robles Cabernet Sauvignon so exciting. As it evolves, barrel bouquet notes of hazelnut, cocoa, and roasted coffee are revealed. On the palate, high-toned red berry flavors are underscored by bright acidity and a compelling structure that is both dense and soft.

WINEMAKER'S INSIGHT

The fruit for the Seven Oaks Cabernet Sauvignon is predominantly grown in the estate vineyards located directly opposite the lovely J. Lohr Paso Robles Wine Center, and at two newer sites to the north. The soils vary from gravelly clay loam to limestone-based soils, and the team planted a thoughtful selection of rootstock and clonal combinations to maximize the expression of each site.

AWARDS & DISTINCTIONS

90 Points – Editors' Choice, *Wine Enthusiast*

TECHNICAL DATA

APPELLATION: Paso Robles
COMPOSITION: 80% Cabernet Sauvignon, 7% Petite Sirah, 6% Petit Verdot, 3% Merlot, 4% other red varieties
MATURATION: This wine was aged for 12 months in 22% new, 60-gallon American oak barrels.
CELLARING: Beautifully open and balanced upon release, this wine has the structure to age well for five years or more.

LEARN MORE

Learn more about J. Lohr wines by scanning the image on the left

Taking inspiration from the famed wines of Bordeaux, their goal was to craft supple and appealing Cabernet Sauvignons with lush, generous fruit and velvety textures. To achieve this, Jerry understood early on, what many others discovered later—the land picks the grape.

With its well-drained, gravelly, and sometimes chalky limestone soils, Jerry knew that Paso Robles was ideal for Bordeaux varieties. There, long, sun-kissed days and temperature swings of 45 to 50 degrees from early morning to midday offered perfect conditions for coaxing rich, voluptuous flavors from the grapes. Just as these unique conditions made the flavors sing, they also tamed the tannins, yielding voluminous silky wines that glided across the palate.

When Jerry planted his first vineyards in Paso Robles in 1986, there were just a few dozen wineries in the region. Over the next two years, J. Lohr built a winery in Paso Robles and made the debut vintage of J. Lohr Estates Seven Oaks Cabernet Sauvignon, with then-director of winemaking Jeff Meier, who has been by Jerry's side for over 35 vintages and is president and COO today. With its luxurious flavors of blueberry, cherry, and chocolate, Seven Oaks quickly established itself as a perennial American favorite, introducing millions of wine drinkers to the joy of Paso Robles Cabernet. In the years that followed, the J. Lohr team dedicated itself to introducing the finest modern winegrowing methods, including innovative

TOP: An oak tree framed by J. Lohr's estate grapevines in the Creston District of Paso Robles.

BELOW: A true family-run winery, two dedicated generations of the Lohr family guide the company's day-to-day operations. (Left to right) Lawrence Lohr, co-owner, Steve Lohr, CEO & co-owner, Jerry Lohr, counder, Cynthia Lohr, trade and brand advocate, co-owner.

LEFT: Our Estate-grown Cabernet Sauvignon grapes ripen in one of our Paso Robles vineyards.
Photographs courtesy of J. Lohr Vineyards

farming techniques, cutting-edge irrigation practices, and a passionate commitment to sustainability.

Today, with more than 200 wineries, and more Cabernet Sauvignon grown in the appellation than in any county other than Napa Valley, Paso Robles is recognized as one of the finest winegrowing regions in the world. As Paso Robles has evolved, so has J. Lohr's estate program, which now features more than 2,000 acres of sustainably certified Cabernet vines. From these grapes, J. Lohr's Cabernet portfolio has grown to include the renowned Hilltop Cabernet Sauvignon, and J. Lohr's pinnacle Signature Cabernet Sauvignon—a coveted, limited-production wine that was debuted for Jerry's 80th birthday. Made by acclaimed Red Wines Winemaker Steve Peck—who was named Winemaker of the Year by the San Luis Obispo County wine industry in 2016—these wines are recognized as benchmarks, showing that Paso Robles Cabernet can stand proudly alongside the world's greatest wines.

TOP: The stunning view from Beck Vineyard in Paso Robles.

BELOW: Guests enjoy the inviting patio at the J. Lohr Paso Robles Wine Center on a year-round basis.
Photographs courtesy of J. Lohr Vineyards

J. LOHR
HILLTOP CABERNET SAUVIGNON

GOURMET PAIRINGS

With its gorgeous depth and robust structure, this wine is a perfect complement to rosemary-seasoned ribeye served with garlic roasted potatoes with parsnips and fennel.

TASTING NOTES

The J. Lohr Hilltop is a stunning example of the "dense, but soft" house style of Cabernet Sauvignon that has made J. Lohr famous across the country and around the world. Effusive blackberry and currant aromas are seamlessly integrated with a bouquet of toasted hazelnut and cocoa powder from aging in the finest French oak barrels. On the palate, generous layers of vibrant fruit dominate, gliding to a silky finish.

WINEMAKER'S INSIGHT

The Hilltop Cabernet Sauvignon is grown on a handful of exceptional Paso Robles vineyard sites that are blessed with long summer days of intense sunshine, followed by chilly, ocean-cooled nights in the 50s. The vines are naturally stressed in the dry soils, where the team is able to fine-tune the irrigation to achieve beautifully dark grapes, with luxurious flavors and plush, resolved tannins vintage after vintage.

AWARDS & DISTINCTIONS

93 Points – *Wine Enthusiast*

TECHNICAL DATA

APPELLATION: Paso Robles
COMPOSITION: 95% Cabernet Sauvignon, 4% Malbec, 1% Petit Verdot
MATURATION: This wine was aged for 18 months in 80% new 225-liter French oak, thick-stave barrels.
CELLARING: Though vibrant and voluptuous upon release, this wine has abundant structure to age beautifully for up to a decade.

ORDER OUR WINE

Learn more about J. Lohr wines by scanning the image on the left

J. LOHR
SIGNATURE CABERNET SAUVIGNON

GOURMET PAIRINGS

The deep, rich blue fruit flavors in this epic wine pair sumptuously with Cabernet-braised beef shanks, served with parsnip potato purée.

TASTING NOTES

Complex and profoundly structured, this mesmerizing wine comes from the renowned Beck Vineyard, in the Creston District of Paso Robles. Perched above the fog line at 1,700 feet, and featuring ideal calcareous soils and cooling afternoon winds, this remarkable vineyard yields a wine of unparalleled power and purity, with firm, focused tannins that underscore dazzling layers of blackberry, cassis, graphite, and chocolate.

WINEMAKER'S INSIGHT

The debut Signature Cabernet Sauvignon was originally crafted to honor the 80th birthday of founder Jerry Lohr. Signature represents both a tribute to Jerry's pioneering vision for world-class Paso Robles Cabernet Sauvignon, and the portfolio's pinnacle limited-production wine. His signature on the label reflects the fact that this benchmark wine is a personal statement for Jerry, encompassing his decades of experience and history in a single bottle.

AWARDS & DISTINCTIONS

96 Points – *Wine Enthusiast*
94 Points – JebDunnuck.com

TECHNICAL DATA

APPELLATION: Paso Robles
COMPOSITION: 100% Cabernet Sauvignon
MATURATION: Aged for 17 months in 100% new French oak barrels from coopers Demptos, Marcel Cadet, Nadalie, and Saint Martin.
CELLARING: This wine offers superlative density with a juicy structure. It is crafted to reach an early optimum drinking window within three years of release, with the ability to age profoundly in the cellar for 20 years.

LEARN MORE

Learn more about J. Lohr wines by scanning the image on the left

A true family-owned-and-operated winery, Jerry has been joined at J. Lohr by his three adult children: Steve, Cynthia, and Lawrence Lohr—each of whom is a co-owner, and holds a pivotal day-to-day role at the winery. Like their father, all three have championed the regions that have helped to make J. Lohr famous. As CEO, Steve played a key role in shepherding the successful creation of 11 different sub-AVAs in Paso Robles. Cynthia, J. Lohr's trade and brand advocate, was instrumental in establishing the Paso Robles CAB Collective, an organization dedicated to educating the world on the phenomenal quality of the region's Cabernet Sauvignon and red Bordeaux varieties. Lawrence works alongside Jerry in the company's estate vineyards, and like his siblings, is often "in market" representing the brand.

In addition to J. Lohr's pioneering role bringing Paso Robles Cabernet to the world, the winery has also helped bring the world to Paso Robles. The beautiful and inviting J. Lohr Paso Robles Wine Center has consistently set the standard for vineyard-driven red wines in Paso Robles, drawing wine lovers from around the globe eager to taste J. Lohr's Cabernets and Bordeaux-varietal reds as well as its Pinot Noirs, Rhône-varietal wines, and dazzling whites.

TOP: Lawrence, Jerry, and Steve Lohr join J. Lohr's acclaimed winemaking team among the estate vine rows of Paso Robles.

RIGHT: Legendary vintner Jerry Lohr holds a bottle of his namesake Signature Cabernet Sauvignon—the pinnacle of the J. Lohr portfolio.
Photographs courtesy of J. Lohr Vineyards

71

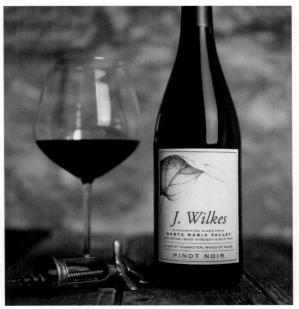

J. Wilkes SANTA MARIA

The story of J. Wilkes begins in one of the oldest appellations in the United States: Santa Maria Valley. Jefferson (Jeff) Wilkes passionately promoted this area in the early 1980s, defining the region that is now known as the heart and soul of Santa Barbara County winemaking. After walking the rows of prestigious Estate Vineyards for twenty years, selling fruit to some of the most famous wineries in California, Jeff launched his namesake label in 2001 and made his final wine in 2010 before his untimely passing that same year.

Inspired by Jeff's vision and moved by their friendship, the Miller family decided to continue the J. Wilkes label as a tribute to Jeff's undying passion for the Santa Maria wine region. Today, Wes Hagen is the J. Wilkes winemaker, a role that was a natural fit after making wine side by side in the same facility with Jeff for several harvests. The two immediately hit it off and shared a common desire to showcase the Santa Maria Valley.

FACING PAGE: Santa Maria's unique transverse valley acts as a funnel, channeling in cool maritime influences and depositing them throughout the wide valley.
Photograph by Adam Felde

TOP LEFT: Jeff Wilkes, the original founder and namesake for the J. Wilkes label.

TOP RIGHT: Our signature Santa Maria Valley Pinot Noir is ready for tasting.
Photographs courtesy of J Wilkes

The brand is dedicated to producing wines from some of the most expressive AVAs in the Central Coast and focuses on the region, the diversity, and typicity of soils. The ultimate goal is to craft wines from the highest quality fruit and let the terroir shine, unfiltered, through the wine.

Santa Maria Valley is a cool-climate wine production area famed for its quality Pinot Noir and Chardonnay since the 1970s. The low-nutrient sandy soil, strong Pacific winds and fog, and sun-kissed slopes of the Tepusquet Bench come together to produce small vines with limited vigor, tiny clusters, and a

J. WILKES SANTA MARIA VALLEY PINOT NOIR

GOURMET PAIRINGS
Cream of chanterelle mushroom soup, with fresh butter, shallots, and a touch of good sherry goes well with this wine. Finish the soup with a golden puff pastry floater.

TASTING NOTES
Aromatics include ripe red berry fruits, cherry pie, kola nut, white pepper, clove, and an intense earthy-spicy-savory-meaty complexity. You'll taste bright, fruity, balanced, and quite complex flavors. The finish shows cherry, rhubarb, and loamy, earthy tannins.

WINEMAKER'S INSIGHT
Wes Hagen's first commercial Santa Maria Pinot Noir was made with the conscious decision to use no new oak in the wine, to show off the fruit and not the French accent. Sixteen months in, 100 percent neutral French oak gives the wine a purity and focus that is purely Santa Maria Valley and Tepesquet Bench—the Grand Cru of Santa Maria viticulture.

AWARDS & DISTINCTIONS
Year's List of Top Best U.S. Pinot Noirs – *Wine & Spirits*
90 points, Best Buy – *Wine & Spirits*
Top 15 Pinot Noirs in CA – Gear Patrol
91 points, Gold Medal – Tastings.com
Gold Medal – San Francisco Chronicle Wine Competition
Served to dignitaries in Washington D.C. at the Nordic Leaders State Dept. luncheon, hosted by Secretary Kerry

TECHNICAL DATA

APPELLATION: Santa Maria Valley
COMPOSITION: 100% Pinot Noir
MATURATION: Aged 16 months in elevage.
CELLARING: Drink now or hold for the next seven to 10 years.

LEARN MORE

Visit our website by scanning the image on left

rare combination of verve and elegance. J. Wilkes produces Pinot Blanc, Chardonnay, and Pinot Noir from the Santa Maria Valley.

Petitioned in 1997 by Wes Hagen and approved in 2001, the Santa Rita Hills are a unique series of east-west coastal valleys that channel fierce winds and dense fog. The result of the sandy soils and cool-climate Pinot Noir production is impressive: tiny berries, dense color, and wines that are famed and sought-after for big style, acid structure, and aging potential. Soils began developing around 12 million years BCE when this area was first thrust out of the Pacific Ocean by a massive tectonic event.

Deep and intensely hard, the soils of Paso Robles Highlands District are younger than what you would find in Santa Maria Valley or Santa Rita Hills. The land has been eroded from geologic parent material formed in the Pleistocene and Old Pliocene—that's

TOP: Winemaker, Wes Hagen, checking grape quality before harvest.

LEFT: Some of the rich soils found in the Paso Robles Highlands District area help sustain strong vines.
Photographs by Makers & Allies

75

five to 10 million years BCE. These soils tend to be alluvial and less acidic than the other two AVAs and are associated with the La Panza Range and the Simmler, Monterey, and Paso Robles formations.

Rising to more than 2,000 feet in some places, this district has the highest elevation of any Central Coast wine production locale, along with the largest diurnal temperature shifts. There is a 50-degree average difference between daytime highs and nighttime lows. J. Wilkes produces Cabernet Sauvignon, Zinfandel, and Lagrein from this land.

The J. Wilkes label celebrates and honors Jeff's life and the bounty of both Santa Maria and Paso Robles through its memorable wines.

TOP: J. Wilkes' proprietors are fifth generation California farmers. Stephen Miller (CEO), Marshall Miller (VP of Operations) and Nicholas Miller (VP Sales & Marketing)
Photograph by Chris Leshinsky

LEFT: Wes Hagen, J. Wilkes winemaker
Photograph by Makers & Allies

J. WILKES PASO ROBLES HIGHLANDS DISTRICT CABERNET SAUVIGNON

GOURMET PAIRINGS

Try a dry-rubbed Moroccan-spiced Colorado rack of lamb with a side of two-year aged Vella Jack potatoes au gratin. Or serve with a nice pile of Israeli couscous with hints of cumin and mint.

TASTING NOTES

Aromatics include black plum, currant, cassis, and ripe black cherry with hints of cocoa nibs, toffee, and cedar. The flavor profile is fruity, juicy, and ripe on the attack—medium body with a rare combination of dense, delicious fruit notes and also a sense of balance and elegance. The long finish is bright and fruity with dust minerality.

WINEMAKER'S INSIGHT

Picked to show richness, ripeness, depth, and complexity, this wine is under 14 percent alcohol, which is quite a feat for modern Paso Robles red wine. Plummy, red and blackberry fruits dominate with strong hints of black cherry and cassis. The wine was fermented on the skins for almost three weeks at a cooler temperature to maintain fresh, aromatic, primary fruit character and an impressive mid-palate and long finish.

AWARDS & DISTINCTIONS

Gold Medal – *San Francisco Chronicle*
93 points – Tasting Panel

TECHNICAL DATA

APPELLATION: Paso Robles Highlands District
COMPOSITION: 85% Cabernet Sauvignon Clone 4, 15% Lagrein
MATURATION: Aged 16 months in elevage.
CELLARING: Drink now, or hold for the next five to seven years, maybe longer.

ORDER OUR WINE

Learn more about J. Wilkes wines by scanning the image the on left

Kaleidos PASO ROBLES

Steve Martell's passion for wine began during his college years at University of California Santa Cruz where he graduated in agro-ecology and biology with an emphasis on organic viticulture.

Time spent with friends enjoying a bottle of wine inspired Martell to establish Kaleidos, which pays homage to his mother's store called Kaleidoscope in Kalamazoo, where Martell grew up. He relates a kaleidoscope's light and colors that unite to create unique images to the vines that combine the elements of soil and sunlight to develop distinctive fruit characteristics.

In 2004, Martell acquired the 24-acre property in the rolling hills of Paso Robles's Willow Creek District on the west side. With his wife Heather and family, he parked his Airstream trailer on the property, rolled up his sleeves, and planted about 2,500 vines on a little more than an acre, with more planting planned in the near future. While waiting for the vines to mature, Martell sourced fruit from Paso Robles' prized vineyards.

With a minuscule annual production of 500 cases, Kaleidos' focus is on Rhône varieties, blends of Grenache, Syrah, and Mourvedre, wines that are bold, complex, and age-worthy. Amongst the whites, the portfolio includes Grenache Blanc and Albariño.

Martell's consistent attention to detail can be tasted with just one memorable sip at the contemporary tasting room in the hip industrial hub of Tin City.

FACING PAGE: Sun rising over the Kaleidos Estate Vineyard in the heart of the Willow Creek District, Paso Robles.

ABOVE LEFT: Harvest time for these Syrah grapes which are carefully hand picked into half-ton picking bins.

ABOVE RIGHT: Beautiful glass of our flagship GSM blend Morpheus.
Photographs by Steve Martell

Michael Gill Cellars PASO ROBLES

As a vintner, dentist, and international hunter, Michael Gill has attained a stature in his endeavors few people can achieve in a lifetime.

A tasting at Michael Gill Cellars is an unforgettable experience. You are welcomed by the sign stating, "Please do not feed or touch the animals." Initially, one might think the sign relates to the friendly Russian wolfhounds that reign in the tasting room. Then the visitor will realize that the sign is not in deference to the Bolzois but to the myriad of animals from around the world that have garnered Dr. Gill the prestigious Safari Club Top Ten Award, among numerous other awards.

The journey of winemaking started in 1998 when the first Syrah was planted on the estate. Now after two decades of toil, there are 10 varietals grown on 15 acres. Dr. Gill has a unique attitude for selecting which varietals to plant, with a focus on newer ones to the state like Counoise. The wine is a constant award winner, being the Best Microwinery Red Wine awarded by the California State Wine Competition and receiving 99 points in a later state competition.

FACING PAGE: Viewing the tasting room and patio from the syrah vineyard planted in 1998; the patio looks over the Syrah and adjacent vineyards in the undulating hills.

ABOVE: Hundred-year-old oak trees welcome you to the tasting room.
Photographs Courtesy of Michael Gill Cellars

Other varietals such as Vermentino, Viognier, Primitivo, Tannat, Alicante Bouschet, Negrette and Zinfandel soon joined the winery's portfolio. Grown on a steep south-facing slope, Tempranillo, one of the original clones from Spain, is a constant winner, receiving Best of All Red Wines from Jerry Mead's NWIWC and earning 99 points.

81

BLACK TIE SYRAH

GOURMET PAIRINGS
Pair with hearty meats such as prime rib, elk, or venison medallions.

TASTING NOTES
The dry-farmed Syrah has intense berry flavors with nuances of black pepper, cardamom, vanilla cola, and black licorice. The finish displays crunchy, dusty tannins, moderate oak, and of course, the Paso Robles terroir.

WINEMAKER'S INSIGHT
Great care is taken to assure the fruit is given every opportunity to be textbook perfect. As all winemakers say, "the wine is made in the field." With the calcareous soil and daily temperature swings of 50 degrees from the heat of the day to the cool of the night, the fruit will get concentrated berry flavor and beautiful acids.

AWARDS & DISTINCTIONS
99 points – Jerry Mead's NWIWC
Gold & double gold medals – California State Fair, Orange County Fair, and Central Coast Wine Competition

TECHNICAL DATA

APPELLATION: Willow Creek AVA
COMPOSITION: 100% Syrah
MATURATION: Aged 16 to 24 months.
CELLARING: The Syrah is ready to drink when released and will be excellent for five to 10 years.

LEARN MORE

Learn more about Michael Gill Cellars by scanning image on left

The backbone of the estate winery is the initially planted Syrah, lush with layered dark fruits with a velvety finish, that has garnered annual Best of Class awards not only in the U.S., but also by the Berlin International Wine Competition in every year entered.

Michael Gill wines are produced from estate fruit—no grapes are bought, no grapes are sold. All varietals are dry farmed, decreasing yield but concentrating the fruit flavors. Old World methods are used, and quality, not quantity, is the focus with an annual case production of a mere 1,000 to 1,200 cases.

It's a family-run operation at Michael Gill Cellars where you will likely see Dr. Gill (or his children) behind the counter, or friendly staff to make your tasting experience more than memorable.

TOP: Our tasting room is like a French hunting lodge; it's a comfortable setting looking out at the Syrah and Tempranillo fields.
Photograph by Jack von Eberstein

MIDDLE & RIGHT: 2018 was another award-winning year.
Photographs Courtesy of Michael Gill Cellars

Monochrome Wines PASO ROBLES

In a region known for big bold red wines, Monochrome stands out as the only winery in Paso Robles dedicated exclusively to white wines. Appropriately named for its "one color," the name also references black-and-white—or monochrome—photography, which some people dismiss as less complex and interesting than color yet can result in some of the most artistic and memorable images. Similarly, some people dismiss white wines as simple and one-dimensional, yet fine white wines can have as much character and complexity as the best reds, and are arguably more challenging to make. That's the inspiration for winemakers Dave McGee and Riley Hubbard.

Noticing that white wines were being underserved in the area, both literally and figuratively, McGee set out on a mission to craft a portfolio of white wines with the same level of effort, thought, and passion that most producers reserve for their very best red wines.

The team produces blends from grapes such as Chardonnay, Sauvignon Blanc, Marsanne, Roussanne, Viognier, Albariño, Chenin Blanc, and Grenache Blanc. Monochrome's first vintage was 2016, with fruit sourced from different microclimates along the entire Central Coast, from vineyards ranging from Arroyo Seco to Santa Barbara.

Monochrome's intimate tasting room is located in Tin City, Paso Robles' hip enclave. Individual and educational group tastings for up to ten people are held by appointment only and are led by the winemaker. Here white wine aficionados can experience wines that are as flavorful, complex, and interesting as the best reds.

FACING PAGE: The Monochrome label signifies our winery's commitment to only white wines.
Photograph by Dave McGee

ABOVE LEFT: Winemaker Dave McGee assesses each barrel during the fermentation and aging of Monochrome's wines.
Photograph by Erin McGee

ABOVE RIGHT: Monochrome's small tasting room is set up for personal and educational tastings with the winemaker, for groups up to 10 people.
Photograph by Dave McGee

Mystic Hills Vineyard SAN MIGUEL

Going from film editing to winemaking is a long stretch. But for Academy Award-wining film editor, Joel Cox, the extension was natural. He applies the same meticulous and diligent approach to winemaking as he does to a well-crafted movie scene. Cox, who has worked with Hollywood legend Clint Eastwood on pretty much all of his films, is honored to receive an Oscar for the film *Unforgiven*.

For a relative newcomer the winery has gathered numerous awards for its Bordeaux-style blends. Starting with their very first release, Unforgiven (inspired by the film) won Best in Class and a Gold Medal at the San Francisco Chronicle Wine Competition.

Mystic Hills' hand-crafted wines showcase the special terroir that make Paso Robles and California's Central Coast so unique. The winery's Platinum and Gold medal winning red wines, Rosé and Sauvignon Blanc, are outstanding examples of impressive Bordeaux-style wines produced from the San Miguel region of Paso Robles appellation. For Cox and his team, it's a family affair and a hands-on approach to winemaking that can take up to three years from grape to bottle. However, for vineyard management and farming the family relies on Keith Roberts. "My farmer, he's the backbone," Cox comments on the veteran with more than 40 years of experience.

The winery hosts several events throughout the year, including Movie Night with Joel Cox, as well as wine club members pick-up parties, new releases parties, and winemaker dinners.

FACING PAGE: Mystic Hills Vineyard has wines that showcase the special terrior and climate that make Paso Robles and California's Central Coast so unique.

ABOVE: Winemaking is a family affair for Joel, Judy, and family at Mystic Hills Vineyard.
Photographs courtesy of Mystic Hills

OpoloVineyards PASO ROBLES

Set in the picturesque rolling hills near Paso Robles, Opolo Vineyards is made up of nearly 300 acres of vines. The expansive swath of land makes it inclusive of a wide range of soil types, climates, and provides great growing potential. A number of varietals flourish here, including Syrah, Malbec, Sangiovese, Tempranillo, Chardonnay, Zinfandel, and Pinot Noir.

Started by neighbors Rick Quinn and Dave Nichols, the winery began with its first vintage in 1999. Today, Rick and Dave run Opolo Vineyards with the help of General Manager Scott Welcher, Winemakers Chris Rougeot and James Schreiner, Vineyard Manager Greg Perez, and Head Distiller Paul Quinn. The small team is hands-on, and is involved in each part of the business, including vineyard contracts, farming practices, winemaking, marketing, and events. The Opolo crew has worked hard over the years to ensure that guests feel welcome, comfortable, and like they are part of the Opolo family.

Starting with the passion in the vineyard, the team carefully monitors each lot of grapes in order to produce the highest quality fruit possible. Great wine begins in the vineyard and everyone works to sustainably farm the grapes. From there, the process continues with the production team and the winemaking steps. Here, extreme attention to detail and finesse is used in crafting consistent, elegant wines. When visiting the Westside Vineyard, guests are able to see the land, learn about the winemaking process, and enjoy great wines, food, and friends.

Located in Paso Robles, the Tasting Room has humble beginnings as a metal tractor barn in the middle of the Westside Vineyard property. In 2017, the

FACING PAGE: View from the Hilltop overlooking the estate vineyard, Paso Robles Willow Creek District AVA, and beyond to the Pacific Ocean.
Photograph by Alyssa Poland Photography

ABOVE: Guests toast to good wine, great company, and amazing views.
Photograph by Oak & Barrel Photography

tasting room was remodeled using refurbished barrel staves, recycled copper tops, and lighting fixtures with reclaimed wine barrel hoops. The same charming metal tractor barn remains, however, with glass roll-up doors and walls covered in a rusty brown corrugated steel.

Used for Opolo events, private tastings, and large groups on the weekends, the Barrel Room is an extension of the Tractor Barn and lined in oak barrels with three dropdown chandeliers. A small distance from the main hospitality area is the aptly named Hilltop. It's an expansive grass lawn that overlooks the property and a wide view of the Westside, Willow Creek AVA. Opolo hosts an array of events and gatherings throughout the year, including the famous annual Harvest Dinner and Grape Stomp— not to be missed. Guests can partake in an on-site lamb roast, grape stomp, dancing, and a toast to the successful harvest with Opolo's closest friends and club members.

Tucked away in the rolling hills of the vineyard and oak trees, The Inn at Opolo is a three-suite bed and breakfast. It has more of an Adriatic coastline influence and pronounced Old World feel. Warm and welcoming, the Inn is an extension of the warm hospitality offered at all points of contact at Opolo.

TOP: An expansive patio outside the Opolo Tasting Room invites guests to enjoy fire-roasted pizzas with a glass of wine.
Photograph by Oak & Barrel Photography

BELOW LEFT: Opolo's annual Harvest Dinner & Grape Stomp, where friends from around the country gather to stomp grapes, dance, and enjoy an abundance of food and wine.
Photograph by Oak & Barrel Photography

BELOW RIGHT: Co-owners Rick Quinn and Dave Nichols
Photograph by A. Blake Photography

OPOLO MOUNTAIN ZINFANDEL

GOURMET PAIRINGS

Opolo's own Pizza Bueno is a hand-tossed, fire-roasted pizza topped with caramelized onions, mushrooms, and grilled chicken over Bren's seasoned white sauce with mozzarella and Parmesan cheese. The combination of flavors and aromas pair perfectly, accentuating the earthier notes of the Opolo Mountain Zinfandel.

TASTING NOTES

This is a quintessential Paso Robles Zinfandel, decadently rich and fruit forward. It opens with rich aromas of raspberry, rhubarb, and Bing cherry with hints of vanilla, cedar, and tea leaf. Flavors of dark plum and cherry are married with silky smooth tannins that lead into a long and satisfying finish.

WINEMAKER'S INSIGHT

The grapes for this wine are sourced from Opolo's vineyards in Paso Robles, an appellation justly famous for producing intense fruit-forward Zinfandels. The climate of these Westside vineyards are characterized by slightly cooler growing conditions due to coastal temperatures and austere soils that produce a fruit with exceptional varietal character and expression.

AWARDS & DISTINCTIONS

93 points – *Wine Enthusiast*

TECHNICAL DATA

APPELLATION: Paso Robles
COMPOSITION: 100% Zinfandel
MATURATION: The wine is aged on a combination of French and American oak for 10 months.
CELLARING: Drink now or enjoy five to 10 years later.

LEARN MORE

Visit our website by scanning the image on the left

Pomar Junction Vineyard & Winery PASO ROBLES

The Merrill family's agricultural heritage and grape-growing history in California's central coast dates back a solid nine generations. After nearly 30 years of growing grapes for many of the finest wineries in California, ranging from ultra-premium small producers to the largest international brands, the Merrills decided to take the leap and produce their own wines.

They purchased the property in 2002 and breathed new life into the existing 40 acres, planting another 56 acres by the next year. In addition to the family estate, the finest blocks of grapes from Santa Barbara and Monterey counties were selected from vineyards managed by a sister firm, Mesa Vineyard Management, Inc. Today, all the wines that Pomar Junction Vineyard & Winery produce are exclusively farmed by the Merrills, who believe that control—from planting and pruning through harvest, fermentation, and cellaring—is critical for success.

Pomar Junction gets its name from several sources. One is obvious: The roads that intersect on the property are El Pomar Drive and South El Pomar Road. The second is that the area has long been known as El Pomar, which led to the sub AVA in the Paso Robles AVA of the Pomar Junction District. The third has a personal connection to the Merrill family, with general manager Matt Merrill's great-grandfather, George Grigg, having been a railroad engineer who worked the Sierra Nevada mountain range. Templeton, where Pomar Junction is located, has also historically been a train town.

FACING PAGE: Merlot grapes hanging on the vine with the Pomar Junction Caboose and Boxcar in the background.
Photograph by Brandon Stier

ABOVE: The view from the deck of the tasting room towards the west with the vineyard and vintage truck near the train tracks.
Photograph by Matthew Browne

93

POMAR JUNCTION CROSSING GSM

GOURMET PAIRINGS

Rack of lamb is an excellent pairing with the Pomar Junction Crossing GSM. The rich earthiness and hints of cigar tobacco complement the flavor of the lamb.

TASTING NOTES

This classic Rhône blend displays a floral nose with hints of black currant, black cherry, blueberry, and a hint of leather and tobacco. A savory mouthfeel is supported by flavors of red and black fruits and sweet spices, with a distinctive lingering finish of supple tannins.

WINEMAKER'S INSIGHT

The grapes which are SIP certified, are gown in a sustainable manner in the El Pomar district of Paso Robles. Linne Calado soils on southwest-facing slopes, combined with Templeton Gap cooling breezes, help produce ultra-premium wine grapes. Extended cold soak pre-fermentation helps extract out the color and flavors of this elegant wine.

AWARDS & DISTINCTIONS

94 points – *Wine Advocate*

TECHNICAL DATA

APPELLATION: El Pomar District, Paso Robles
COMPOSITION: Syrah 42%, Mourvèdre 33%, Grenache 25%
MATURATION: Aged 19 months in oak barrels, 30 percent of which are new French.
CELLARING: Can be enjoyed now, but will cellar nicely for seven years or more.

LEARN MORE

Learn more about Pomar Junction Vineyards & Wines

Today, GM Matt is in charge of the brand, while wife Nicole oversees the wine club and acts as compliance manager. A version of Pomar Junction's first vintage, a Cabernet Sauvignon, was consumed at their wedding a year after they started producing wines. Matt's parents, founders and owners Dana and Marsha Merrill, are very much active not only with Pomar Junction, but in and around the local wine industry and community—Dana has chaired the California Association of Winegrape Growers as a representative of Paso Robles, served two terms on the Paso Robles Wine Country Alliance and Monterey County Vintners and Growers Association boards, and was honored as the 2012 Paso Robles Wine Industry Person of the Year. Bruce Jordan manages the vineyard, while head winemaker Jim Shumate teaches at the Cal Poly Wine and Viticulture Department, where he piloted winemaking and the transition to a new state-of-the-art facility at the university set to open in 2020.

TOP: The Cabernet Sauvignon vines pictured on the morning of their harvest. Pomar Junction is full of majestic views.
Photograph by Matt Merrill

RIGHT: The Merrill Family (L to R): Matt Merrill, Ethan Merrill, Nicole Merrill, Eleanor Merrill, Marsha Merrill, Dana Merrill
Photograph by Allyson Magda

A lifelong dedication to learning and adopting the smartest techniques has propelled Pomar Junction to dedicate itself to sustainability, achieving certification in the SIP (Sustainability In Practice) program within the Central Coast Vineyard Team. Keeping with the sustainable theme, a 1920s farmhouse on the property was converted into the tasting room in 2008, with the winery itself following in 2011. In 2013 alone, they produced 8,500 cases.

Wine-lovers seek out Pomar Junction's Chardonnay, Viognier, Grenache Blanc, Syrah Rosé, Merlot, Pinot Noir, Zinfandel, Cabernet Sauvignon, Tempranillo, Petite Sirah, Grenache Noir, and various blends. Pomar Junction offers an extensive Wine Club with fun "pick-up parties" at the nearby family 285-acre ranch as well as the Pomar Junction Vineyard. We offer private tastings in our family wine cellar which holds 1,000 cases of wine. We also offer vineyard tours around our various properties in the El Pomar District of Paso Robles. Our tours and tastings offer various Pomar Junction wines while describing its sustainability practices, sharing the history of the winery, and learning about everything that happens while turning grapes into wine.

TOP: Early morning Viognier hand harvest.

ABOVE: The Family Wine Cellar at Pomar Junction Vineyard holds more than 1,000 cases of wine and is an impressive place to host private tastings.
Photographs by Matt Merrill

TRAIN WRECK

GOURMET PAIRINGS

Train Wreck pairs perfectly with the smokiness of a filet mignon, as its silky tannins and robust dark fruit complement decadent sauces and pepper notes.

TASTING NOTES

Train Wreck is a collision of six different varieties that highlight the Paso Robles El Pomar District growing region. This wine is no accident, as it was carefully crafted to exude layers of intense flavors such as black currants and dark stone fruits while exhibiting soft, velvety tannins.

WINEMAKER'S INSIGHT

The grapes which are SIP certified, are gown in a sustainable manner in the El Pomar district of Paso Robles. Linne Calado soils on southwest-facing slopes, combined with Templeton Gap cooling breezes, help produce ultra-premium wine grapes. Extended cold soak pre-fermentation helps extract out the color and flavors of this elegant wine.

AWARDS & DISTINCTIONS

Double Gold – Finger Lakes International Wine Competition
Best of Class – San Francisco Chronicle Wine Competition

TECHNICAL DATA

APPELLATION: El Pomar District, Paso Robles
COMPOSITION: 25% Petite Sirah, 22% Merlot, 15% Cabernet Sauvignon, 15% Syrah, 15% Zinfandel, 8% Mourvedre
MATURATION: Aged 21 months in oak barrels, 35 percent New French and American oak.
CELLARING: Can be enjoyed now but will cellar nicely for 10 years or more.

ORDER OUR WINE

Visit our wine store by scanning the image to left

Red Soles Winery & Distillery   PASO ROBLES

Much like grapes take time to reach a prime level of ripeness, Randy and Cheryl Phillips waited for the ideal time to try winemaking. The couple had been growing premium wine grapes in Paso Robles since the 1980s, and before that had spent years in Napa Valley and Spain, but it wasn't until 2004 that Cheryl held back a bin of their own Zinfandel and Petite Sirah grapes. She and Randy jumped in, literally feet first, crushing the grapes themselves and emerging with soles stained a deep crimson—inspiring the label they would soon create.

Initially, the Phillipses were content to focus on the farming side of wine, supplying grapes to several large wineries from their 100 acres. Even today, only a small percentage of what they grow—with the help of longtime vineyard employees Carmelo Hernandez and Avalino Santos Rosales—gets turned into Red Soles wine; the rest of the grapes are sold to large wineries, most of whom Randy and Cheryl have been doing business with for more than 20 years. But the glut of wine grapes produced in the mid-2000s spurred them to open their own winery and help weather the pricing downturn. The duo soon found they enjoyed the creativity and connections they were making. While they will always love being part of a wine grape's journey from dust to vine and vine to barrel, they decided to also grow their own label.

Today, the Oakdale vineyard produces entirely estate-grown wines, which are crushed and pressed at the Phillips' facility with their own equipment, and then barreled down in the storage room at the back of the property. The Willow Creek appellation, with its cooler daytime temperatures, coastal

FACING PAGE: Guests are greeted by beautiful gardens as they approach the tasting room and often stay to enjoy a glass and the views before continuing.

TOP LEFT: High school sweethearts, Randy and Cheryl Phillips share a moment to celebrate the 10th anniversary of Red Soles Winery after a spectacular winemaker's dinner party.

TOP RIGHT: The rich, ruby tone of Garnacha sparkles in the sunshine.
Photographs by Gina Cinardo

GARNACHA

GOURMET PAIRINGS

Paella is an exceptionally good pairing. Spiced, flavorful seafood and rich bites of sausage nestled in a savory skillet of seasoned rice are a perfect complement to a bottle of Garnacha.

TASTING NOTES

Cherry-juice aromas meet rounded star anise and spice on the nose of this estate, single-vineyard wine. There is a chalky elegance on the mid-palate from the chalk and limestone shale soils of the vineyard that frames flavors of red fruit and orange rind. It finishes with giant, lingering vanilla notes. This is a powerful wine that offers medium alcohol, balanced acidity, and overall deep raspberry and wild strawberry flavors.

WINEMAKER'S INSIGHT

The old-school, double goblet headtrained system is used, which pairs nicely with the chalk and limestone shale soils. It allows unobstructed airflow through the vines and fruit clusters for even maturity in the fruit, and limits the amount of fruit the vine will produce. The majority of Garnacha grown in Spain is also head trained. A head trained vine has no wires and can look like a small tree in the vineyard with several extensions (branches) coming off the trunk of the vine. This is key in making the Estate Garnacha one of the best wines at Red Soles.

AWARDS & DISTINCTIONS

Best of Class, Gold Medal – California State Fair
Best of Class – Central Coast Wine Competition
Gold Medal – San Francisco Chronicle Wine Competition
Gold Medal – Orange County Fair

TECHNICAL DATA

APPELLATION: Paso Robles, Willow Creek District
COMPOSITION: 100% Garnacha
MATURATION: This wine is aged 15 months in American oak.
CELLARING: This wine pours great now, or will age well tucked in your cellar for the next eight years.

LEARN MORE

Learn more our wines by scanning image on left

breezes, and limestone-rich soil, imparts a distinct minerality to the wines, which include Chardonnay, Viognier, Syrah, Cabernet Sauvignon, Zinfandel, Petite Sirah, Tempranillo, Garnacha, and Mourvedre. That original namesake blend that Randy and Cheryl first made that fateful day has proved so popular that they still bottle it under the name Kick-Off.

In 2010, Tiffani Morones joined Red Soles as its tasting room manager. She introduces visitors to not only the award-winning wines, but also to "Patience My Dear," the custom, handcrafted Arnold Holstein still from Germany that the winery acquired in 2013. Red Soles was among the first wineries in Paso Robles to secure a DSP (Distilled Spirits Plant) permit, which allows them to make liquor, and lucky visitors can watch Patience process wine into fine brandy.

TOP: Our 100-acre Miracles Ranch, with its chalky limestone and afternoon breeze, sits in the heart of the Willow Creek District of Paso Robles.
Photograph by Brittany App

MIDDLE: The hundred-acre property grows a variety of grapes; everything poured in the tasting room is made from the fruit grown here.
Photograph by Gina Cinardo

RIGHT: The German-made still, "Patience My Dear," transforms wine into craft brandy at Red Soles Winery & Distillery. Our offerings include both traditional and flavored brandies.
Photograph by Gina Cinardo

Seven Angels Cellars TEMPLETON

The single biggest influence on the creation and day-to-day operations of Seven Angels Cellars is simple: family. It's what inspired it, fuels it, and gives it a promise of a bright future.

Started by Greg and Pamela, the winery has its roots in the founders' childhoods. Each of them has had a lifelong passion for food and wine that began with their upbringings. Pamela was raised in a family of foodies and cooks, and took college courses in oenology as a young adult. Later she would own a catering business, teach cooking classes in Hollywood, and work on a TV show as an assistant home economist. Greg grew up in rural Southern California, surrounded by neighbors who were no strangers to grape growing. His natural curiosity and patient neighbor allowed him to spend many hours in the vineyard, soaking it all in. Stationed in the Bay Area during his stint in the Coast Guard, Greg was in close proximity to some of the state's best vineyards. He explored and educated himself on all things wine. When the couple got married, Greg continued to express his desire and passion to become a winemaker, and they both agreed it was time. In 2009, Greg and Pamela contracted their first grapes for Seven Angels and made a Petite Sirah.

FACING PAGE: The sign at the entrance to Seven Angels Cellars tasting room is handcrafted from wine barrel bands.

TOP: Owners Greg and Pamela Martin sampling the Grace red blend and Zinfandel. Keeping close tabs on the flavors ensures the consistency in quality.
Photographs by Victoria Schmidt

Seven Angels Cellars takes its name from the blending of Greg and Pamela's families. When they met, Greg had four children and Pamela had three; together, they have seven. Hence the name. Family is a priority in their lives, and all decisions made center around their love for family and time spent together. That care and passion comes through in the wine. Handcrafted with

103

a close attention to detail, all of the wines are food-friendly and approachable in flavor integration. They possess distinct characteristics and are offered at a common-sense price point. Varietals include Syrah, Zinfandel, Cabernet Sauvignon, Chardonnay, Viognier andGrenache Blanc, as well as red and white blends.

As a family-owned business, the team is 100 percent committed to maintaining high quality, delicious wines that people will want to share and talk about. With Greg and Pamela as the owners and Greg as the winemaker, they also have a couple of key members on their team who make it all possible: Stephanie Spurlock, office and wine club manager; and Kristen Cecil, who oversees marketing and sales.

You can stop by and see the team at the vineyard and tasting room—on the land that charmingly began as a dairy farm in the 1950s. Now a top-tier vineyard ranch, the property was well researched before the Martins took over. Two dozen sample pits

TOP LEFT: View of the tasting room and the Grenache block of vines as you drive up the entry road.

BELOW LEFT: The upper pond, lined with Salinas River rock, is the place to enjoy a glass of wine and 360-degree views of the vineyards, oaks, and river.

ABOVE: Greg Martin at sunrise in the vineyard.
Photographs by Victoria Schmidt

CHOSEN ONE

GOURMET PAIRINGS

The big, bold flavors of this blend lend themselves to being paired with hearty, robust food. Take a look at the winery website for a Sicilian Sausage Soup that goes wonderfully with this wine. Hearty Bolognese sauce over al dente pasta, or chicken marsala will also pair well.

TASTING NOTES

This blend of 50 percent Grenache, 33 percent Mourvèdre, and 17 percent Syrah is quite a delicious and full package. The nose is pretty yet also dense and brawny, with aromas of baked black plum, wild blackberry, leather, sagebrush, and lightly roasted coffee. There is lots of chalky texture on the palate and a pointed acidity, presenting exotic flavors of plum, mulberry, pepper spice, and a touch of nutmeg

WINEMAKER'S INSIGHT

The Syrah (trellised) is from the Willow Creek District, the Mourvedre (trellised) and Grenache (head-trained) are grown in the Templeton Gap, which is the highest elevation in the gap. Moist sea breezes help cool the mornings and evenings. All three varietals were brought in at dawn; most bins are cold-soaked to achieve optimal extraction of color. The wine is fermented in small-lot open bins, receiving several daily punchdowns throughout fermentation.

AWARDS & DISTINCTIONS

93 points – *Wine Enthusiast*
Gold Medal – *Orange County Fair*

TECHNICAL DATA

APPELLATION: Paso Robles
COMPOSITION: 50% Grenache, 33% Mourvedre, 17% Syrah. The percentages are subject to change each year to maintain the proper flavor profile.
MATURATION: Grenache and Mourvedre are aged 22 months in ten French oak barrels, and Syrah 22 months in Russian oak barrels.
CELLARING: Delicious upon release and will age beautifully for up to 15 years.

ORDER OUR WINE

Visit our website by scanning the image to left

ZINFANDEL

GOURMET PAIRINGS

The spice and pepper of this Zinfandel pairs well with robust Southern Italian dishes, sweet and sticky baby-back ribs, and meatball subs with melted provolone.

TASTING NOTES

Coming from a vineyard named after the patron saint of night watchmen, this wine offers luxurious purple aromas of blackberry-vanilla sauce and dark chocolate. The palate is sticky and singing with coffee, milk chocolate, and dried cherries, showing plenty of deep tannins and boisterous acidity that will make this bottling last a while.

WINEMAKER'S INSIGHT

St. Peter of Alcantara Vineyard is one of the steepest head-trained zinfandel vineyards in San Luis Obispo County. Zinfandel ripens at an uneven rate, with clusters ready at differing times. Watchfulness is key and careful sorting post-harvest is instrumental in maintaining the quality and consistency. Picked before dawn to take advantage of the cool mornings, the grapes are brought straight to the sorting table.

AWARDS & DISTINCTIONS

92 points – *Wine Enthusiast*

TECHNICAL DATA

APPELLATION: Paso Robles, Templeton Gap
COMPOSITION: 94% Zinfandel, 6% Petite Sirah
MATURATION: Aged 20 months in 50 percent new Hungarian oak.
CELLARING: Delicious now, and ages well eight-plus years.

ORDER OUR WINE

Visit our wine store by scanning image on left

were used for optimal analysis in order to plant the best suited grape varietals, and today, Seven Angels is just shy of 26 acres of estate fruit. For a 360-degree view of the vineyards, oaks, and river, head up to the hilltop pond, lined with Salinas river rock. The quaint tasting room has a history in education. There is a 60-foot deck with outstanding eastern and southern vistas, where wine enthusiasts can sit and listen to the sounds of nature. Head inside the tasting room and you'll find a grand piano. Guests are free to sit down and play a tune for all their new friends.

Wine Club release parties happen twice a year with sneak previews of unreleased wines paired with homemade appetizers, prepared by Pamela. Festival participation varies, but you can expect to see Seven Angels at the Atascadero Wine Festival and Mammoth Wine Walk as well as a variety of community and nonprofit events.

TOP: The Seven Angels, Pamela and Greg's children, a blended family, who inspired us to name our winery 7 Angels Cellars. (right to left) David Martin, Kristen Cecil, Casey Weaver, Justin Martin, Kelly Murphy, Greg Martin, Pamela Martin, Sarah Martin, Adam Martin
Photograph by Francesca Marchese

RIGHT: Greg and Pamela enjoy spending time in Long Beach, where they hail from, often attending charity events at historic locations around the city, such as the Bixby Hill Rancho, pictured here.
Photograph by Lisa Diaz

Seven Oxen Estate Wines PASO ROBLES

An industrial enclave is an unlikely place for star-gazing at Seven Oxen Estate's winery and tasting room. However, it's the vineyard located a few miles west that offers the spectacular experience. The estate is named after septem triones (seven plow ox), a Latin term for the seven stars of the Big Dipper constellation, which rotates around the North Star throughout the year like oxen on a threshing floor.

Seven Oxen founders Stephen, Anneke, Patrick, and Adriana Neal were interested in putting down roots on the Central Coast, and finding a piece of land that would remain in the family for generations to come. Their interest in the wine business was sparked by a meeting with Bastien Leduc, who was introduced to the Neals through his wife's family connection. Bastien grew up on his father's organic vineyard in southwest France and experienced winemaking in his homeland and in Australia. His approach to vineyard practices and organic farming aligned with the family's philosophy, and with Bastien on the team, the Neals were assured they had a partner who shared their vision. In 2012, the Neals acquired the property perched atop the rolling hills of Paso Robles' west side, and Bastien came on board as Seven Oxen's Vineyard Manager and Winemaker.

FACING PAGE: Seven Oxen Winery is located in a cluster of industrial buildings just south of Paso Robles. Guests can bring a picnic lunch to enjoy on the patio while they taste wine.

ABOVE: Seven Oxen shares the industrial building it calls home with a distillery, a brewery, and another winery. Located right off of Highway 101, it has excellent visibility and is easily accessible for visitors.
Photographs by Bastien Leduc

Between 2013 and 2016, the Seven Oxen team sold half of their fruit and kept the remainder for their own label. The first four vintages averaged an annual production of 600 cases. The philosophy at Seven Oxen is to produce small lots of artisanal wines from the organically farmed vineyard that bridges the Willow Creek and Templeton Gap appellations.

CASSIDY

GOURMET PAIRINGS

The complex mix of flavors in a Thai red curry pairs perfectly with the vanilla and spice notes of the Grenache-Mourvèdre blend. Serve over confit duck legs on a bed of forbidden rice.

TASTING NOTES

Cassidy is a blend of Grenache and Mourvèdre, but also a blend between California and France: it's ripe and rich like a Californian wine, but also elegant and balanced like a French Rhône. The terroir on the estate vineyard in west Paso Robles allows for this unique balance between ripeness and acidity. A ripe and juicy Grenache delivers strong red fruit flavors and long-lasting mouthfeel, and an earthy and spicy Mourvèdre provides color, tannins, and complexity.

WINEMAKER'S INSIGHT

The Grenache and Mourvèdre fruit come exclusively from the organically farmed estate vineyard in west Paso. The Grenache block has been dry-farmed since 2014. The vines are all head-pruned like most vineyards in southern Rhône (i.e. Châteauneuf du Pape), with a lot of work done by hand during the growing season to enhance maturity and prevent diseases. The grapes are hand-harvested, and then fermented separately in small batches, allowing Winemaker Bastien Leduc to precisely select the perfect composition for Cassidy.

AWARDS & DISTINCTIONS

93 points – *Wine Enthusiast*

TECHNICAL DATA

APPELLATION: Templeton Gap
COMPOSITION: 65% Grenache, 35% Mourvèdre
MATURATION: Grenache is aged 18 months in one-year-old and neutral French oak barrels. Mourvèdre is aged 18 months in one-, two-, and three-year-old French oak barrels. It's bottled in March following harvest and aged 12 to 18 months in both before being released.
CELLARING: Delicious now, but can be cellared for up to eight years.

LEARN MORE

Learn more about our wines

TOP LEFT: Winemaker and Vineyard Manager Bastien Leduc farms the organic 26-acre Estate Vineyard using sustainable practices to ensure the vineyard yields top-quality fruit.
Photograph by Rebecca Leduc

TOP RIGHT: Bastien grew up helping his father on his family's organic vineyard in the southwest of France. He holds a degree in viticulture and oenology as well as in organic agricultural consulting.
Photograph by Mike Larson

BOTTOM LEFT: A 100-year-old barn at the base of the vineyard houses the company's farming equipment and keeps grapes cool during hot harvest days. While there is no wine tasting at the vineyard yet, it's part of the long-term dream for Seven Oxen.
Photograph by Adriana Neal

BOTTOM RIGHT: Bastien learned about winemaking and vineyard management from his father, Claude, at a very young age. Claude visits Bastien from France every winter to lend his palate and assist with blending at Seven Oxen.
Photograph by Adriana Neal

The 130-acre estate includes 26 acres of head-pruned, spur-trained vines planted in nine distinct blocks of Mourvèdre, Zinfandel, Petite Sirah, Grenache, and Tannat. South-facing hillsides, chalky soil, hot sunny days, and cooling afternoon breezes from the coast define the flavor and intensity of the grapes.

Under Leduc's minimalist approach and sustainable farming practices, the vineyards are free of pesticides and chemical fertilizers, and yields are kept low to guarantee the highest quality fruit possible and to ensure the health and longevity of the vines.

Leduc brings a French sensibility in crafting the wines: they are big and bold, yet elegant with finesse and complexity. The focus here is on red wines. The portfolio includes Rhône-style single varietals such as Grenache and Mourvèdre, and the uncommon Tannat (native to southwest France), a deep-hued, tannic wine

not found in many Paso Robles' tasting rooms. The family's philosophy is to produce wines from estate fruit only, so in the typical Grenache Syrah Mourvèdre (GSM) blend, Leduc has used Tannat instead of Syrah, which is not a variety grown on the Seven Oxen property.

Following in the family tradition, Adriana Neal, the winery's general manager, learned about environmental responsibility and organic living from her mom Anneke and about wine from her dad, Stephen. She is joined in the tasting room by manager Nancy Gonzalez. The two offer a personalized tasting experience of Seven Oxen wines. For the Neal family team, the winery is a true labor of love, crafting wines they are proud of and believe in passionately.

The tasting room is open Thursday to Monday from 11 a.m. to 5 p.m. Winery tours and private tastings with the winemaker (including barrel tastings) are by appointment only.

TOP: The interior of the tasting room celebrates the building's industrial design. The aesthetic is clean and simple, like the rest of Seven Oxen's branding.

RIGHT: Seven Oxen is expanding their schedule of events as they settle into their new location. The location provides great opportunities for food trucks and live music, and the stunning sunsets make evening events particularly special.
Photographs by Adriana Neal

TANNAT

GOURMET PAIRINGS

Pair with a Northern Italian-style fennel sausage and red radicchio risotto. The Tannat cuts the rich flavors of the risotto and highlights the flavorful spices of the sausage. You can also use the Tannat to deglaze while cooking.

TASTING NOTES

Seven Oxen's Tannat is bold and robust. Significant tannins are balanced by the varietal's natural spiciness, but make it a wine well-suited for aging. From the first sip, this wine shows deep aromas ranging from macerated plums and cherries to dark chocolate and black licorice. With strong tannins that provide a rich texture and structure, the wine is meant to be enjoyed with food.

WINEMAKER'S INSIGHT

Tannat is most commonly used as a blending grape to provide structure and acidity. Due to the climate in Paso Robles, it's possible to push the maturity of the Tannat grape a bit further. This creates riper, softer tannins and beautiful black fruit aromas while still maintaining a bright acidity, resulting in a delicious and approachable single-varietal wine. Seven Oxen's Tannat is pressed immediately after, or sometimes before, fermentation is complete to avoid over-extraction of tannins.

AWARDS & DISTINCTIONS

91 Points – *Wine Enthusiast*

TECHNICAL DATA

APPELLATION: Templeton Gap
COMPOSITION: 100% Tannat
MATURATION: Aged 18 months in new (30 to 50 percent) and used French oak (50 to 70 percent), depending on the year.
CELLARING: Delicious to drink now, but with a vibrant acidity and tannins, can be cellared for up to eight years.

ORDER OUR WINE

Visit our Wine store by scanning the image to left

TABLAS
CREEK
VINEYARD

Tablas Creek Vineyard PASO ROBLES

When two notable international wine families combine forces to create a California-based operation, you know it's going to be great. Tablas Creek Vineyard, a key pioneer of California's Rhône movement, is a partnership between the Perrin family of Chateau de Beaucastel and the Haas family of Vineyard Brands. Groundbreaking importer Robert Haas first introduced the Perrins' famed Chateauneuf-du-Pape estate to America in the late 1960s. After two decades of traveling, exploring, and tasting together, Haas and the brothers Jean-Pierre and Francois Perrin agreed that the uniquely Mediterranean climate and limestone soils of Paso Robles would produce phenomenal Rhône varieties. And so Tablas Creek was born.

Established in 1989, Tablas Creek Vineyard practices biodynamic farming on a 120-acre, organic estate just over 10 miles from the Pacific Coast. Planted with cuttings from Beaucastel—including Mourvèdre, Syrah, Grenache, Counoise, Roussanne, Marsanne, Grenache Blanc, Viognier, and Picpoul—the land is home to roaming sheep, alpacas, and two endearing guard donkeys. The vineyard is largely dry-farmed and produces wines of depth, power, and elegance.

FACING PAGE: The Tablas Creek tasting room is located at the estate winery, in the heart of the beautiful Paso Robles Adelaida District.

ABOVE LEFT: The tasting room looks into the working winery, unique for its use of large (1200 to 1500 gallon) neutral French oak casks called "foudres".

ABOVE RIGHT: A flock of 200-plus sheep, alpacas, and guard animals is a key piece of Tablas Creek's organic and biodynamic vineyard.
Photographs by Jason Haas

Today Tablas Creek is an established leader of the region and of California's Rhône movement. Run by the next generation of Haases and Perrins, as well as long-time winemaker Neil Collins, the estate's Rhône-style wines and blends balance Old World elegance with California purity of fruit. A visit to the vineyard can include one of the region's most educational tours, or a range of traditional and seated flight tastings that reach back into their extensive wine library, all from some of the most influential names in the wine industry.

Villa San-Juliette Vineyard & Winery PASO ROBLES

The story of Villa San-Juliette isn't quite what you'd expect. It involves a reality show, William Shakespeare, and two wildly creative Hollywood producers. Intrigued? Wait until you try the wine.

It all began in 2005 with a show called *Corkscrewed: The Wrath of Grapes*, a television reality series following the trials and exploits of Ken Warwick and Nigel Lythgoe. The award-winning entertainment producers were on a mission to make their long-held dream of owning a vineyard come to life. Once childhood friends in the backstreets of Liverpool, the pair would grow up to produce the American primetime hit, *American Idol*.

With a success story as big as Ken and Nigel's, it's no surprise that the two have spent their lives creating. Their backgrounds include dancing, choreography, television shows, raising families, and now winemaking. A love of theater is also apparent, as the winery's name pays homage to Romeo and Juliet. Because the architectural design of the villa features many balconies, the owners couldn't help but think of the famous, romantic play. The Tuscan-inspired winery lives up to the beauty—and expectations—of its name.

Located in the Paso Robles Estrella District, Villa San-Juliette boasts 168 acres of breathtaking vineyards yielding a diverse range of estate-grown wines, carefully crafted by winemaker Dan Smith. The award-winning wines are balanced and complex with the richness and intense varietal character that Paso Robles' wines are known for. Vineyard manager Eufemio Saucedo works side by side with Dan to craft 12 varietals and two red blends. They are all are grown and produced on the estate vineyard: Cabernet Sauvignon, Cabernet

FACING PAGE: Winemaker Dan Smith prepares the cellar to welcome the first fruit of the new vintage.

ABOVE: Proprietors Ken and Julie Warwick sip their favorite VSJ wines on the beautiful gardens of Villa San-Juliette.
Photographs by Brandon Stier

VILLA SAN-JULIETTE ROSÉ

GOURMET PAIRINGS
Pairs well with pan-seared herbed quail and wild mushrooms with white truffle-oil risotto.

TASTING NOTES
The Villa San-Juliette Rosé is pleasantly peach-hued with corresponding stone fruit character. With poached apple, apricot, and tuberose on the nose, this wine boosts aromas of spring essence. With aeration, the aromas expand to strawberry cream and raw honey. The palate is equally complex and evolving, with flavors of pear, grapefruit, and ripe nectarine that segue into a crisp, mouthwatering finish.

WINEMAKER'S INSIGHT
The Rosé starts in the vineyard where select rows of red varieties are chosen for early harvest. The grapes are hand-picked then destemmed to press where the juice is held with the skins for two to three hours. After a pale pink color is reached, the fruit is lightly pressed to stainless steel to begin a cold fermentation, which ensures that desirable aromatics are maintained. The fermentation is followed by six months of aging in neutral French oak to soften the acidity and boost creaminess via lees stirring.

AWARDS & DISTINCTIONS
90 points – International Wine Review
89 points – *Wine Enthusiast*
Silver Medal – Central Coast Wine Competition

TECHNICAL DATA

APPELLATION: Paso Robles, Estrella District
COMPOSITION: 76% Grenache, 11% Zinfandel, 8% Petite Sirah, 5% Syrah
MATURATION: Aged in neutral French oak for six months.
CELLARING: Delicious now with cellaring up to two years.

LEARN MORE

Visit our website by scanning the image on left.

Franc, Merlot, Petit Verdot, Malbec, Grenache, Syrah, Petite Sirah, Zinfandel, Alicante Bouschet, Sauvignon Blanc, Pinot Gris, Chorum Red Blend, and Romantique Red Blend.

Villa San-Juliette features year-round fun and events to go with its award-winning wines. Wine club parties happen during the months of March, June, September, and December; and you can catch the Sunday Summer Music Series from May to October. Chef-inspired cooking classes and winemaker dinners are also offered throughout the year. Please contact the winery to get dates and times. Winery and vineyard tours are always available by appointment, Friday to Sunday.

Looking for an impressive venue? The property is a dream location for weddings, receptions, and ceremonies. Group outings are also welcome here, whether for business or pleasure. Enjoy a birthday party with your friends, or reward your management team with a corporate retreat on the open-air patio. The property features several locations for your group to meet, relax, enjoy, and have fun. With stunning views, gorgeous surroundings, and world-class service, your event will undoubtedly be a smash hit.

If you're looking for something a little out of the ordinary, Villa San-Juliette can arrange fun, romantic, or educational estate

TOP: Guests can take in stunning scenery while enjoying food and wine service on the Villa patio.

BELOW: The Villa front doors welcome guests to a gorgeous and spacious Tasting Room.
Photographs by Brandon Stier

experiences. For example, you could surprise the love of your life with the perfect proposal. Or get away from it all with an artisan meal on the patio overlooking the vineyards. You can also opt for a stroll through the vineyard with a vineyard specialist and learn the nuances of what goes into growing and making the wine. Have a better idea? Call the winery and talk to a team member to customize your experience.

The team at Villa San-Juliette is always happy to provide local hotel recommendations, winery suggestions, and offer fine dining recommendations. This gives guests access to local knowledge and opens up the region's best options.

For wine lovers who want to take it to the next level, consider joining the Reserve Cellar Wine Club. You'll get first dibs on the newest releases, including quarterly shipments either to your door or available to grab at one of the popular pickup parties. Dan personally selects Villa San-Juliette's best wines to offer to club members first, and shipments always include

CABERNET SAUVIGNON

GOURMET PAIRINGS

The wine complements garlic and rosemary-roasted New Zealand lamb chops, Okinawa sweet potatoes, minted baby zucchini, pomegranate, and olallieberry reduction.

TASTING NOTES

Villa San-Juliette Cabernet Sauvignon resounds with vivid red fruit notes and robust structure. Aromas of black cherry, anise, and cigar box intermingle with rhubarb, nutmeg, and cedar notes. This ripe, full-bodied wine offers layers of luscious earthy flavors and spiciness. Milk chocolate, wild blackberries, and chanterelle mushrooms move into savory sage and nutmeg. Firm tannins are lifted by a vibrant acidity that augments the wine's long, vanilla bean finish.

WINEMAKER'S INSIGHT

The Cabernet Sauvignon is field blended between clones 4 and 169 during a hand-pick harvest, before it is hand-sorted and destemmed to small-lot stainless steel and concrete vessels. A four-to five-day cold soak takes place for optimum color and flavor concentration before fermentation. Post ferment, the wine sits on skins for extended maceration between 20 and 40 days to ensure ideal structure before pressing. Aging adds richness and depth to the finished wine.

AWARDS & DISTINCTIONS

90 points – Vinous
91 points – International Wine Review
90 points – Robert Parker's Wine Advocate
Best of Class – Double Gold Central Coast Wine Competition

TECHNICAL DATA

APPELLATION: Paso Robles AVA, Estrella District
COMPOSITION: 95% Cabernet Sauvignon, 3% Cabernet Franc, 2% Petit Verdot
MATURATION: Aged 24 to 30 months in 35 percent new French oak and 10 percent new American oak.
CELLARING: Optimum tasting after 3 years cellared, and up to 15 years.

ORDER OUR WINE

Buy our wines by scanning the image on left.

CHORUM RED RESERVE

GOURMET PAIRINGS

Serve with Chorum-glazed pork belly, sage, pecorino polenta, and Brussels sprout chips.

TASTING NOTES

An unconventional blend of eight distinct varieties, the Chorum Red Reserve is a refreshing break from winemaking tradition. Every year, this wine showcases the intensity, the elegance, and the gusto from the vineyard. By combining the dark, juicy Rhône varieties with the red fruit, tannin-driven Bordeaux varieties, this wine offers nuances that both layer and harmonize. Although the blend changes every year to reflect the vintage, each year the Chorum has perfect pitch.

WINEMAKER'S INSIGHT

Simply stated, the Chorum Red blend is a winemaker's dream. The ability to create original flavor profiles by combining the various varieties of our vineyard is a rewarding process that stretches creativity, artistry, and experimentation.

AWARDS & DISTINCTIONS

93 points – *Wine Enthusiast*
Gold Medal – San Francisco Chronicle Wine Competition

TECHNICAL DATA

APPELLATION: Paso Robles AVA, Estrella District
COMPOSITION: 34% Syrah, 24% Grenache, 16% Petite Sirah, 11% Cabernet Sauvignon, 8% Cabernet Franc, 5% Petit Verdot, 1% Zinfandel, 1% Merlot
MATURATION: Aged 30 months in 20 percent new French oak, 10 percent new American oak.
CELLARING: Delicious now but can be cellared up to 10 or 15 years.

LEARN MORE

Learn about our wine club and special offers to our members by scanning the image on the left.

his notes on the wines' vineyard origins and cellar history, as well as suggestions for food pairings and recipes designed by the winery's in-house chef. But the coolest part might just be the access to one-of-a-kind experiences. Imagine lush gardens, expansive vistas, and European-inspired elegance as an extension of your own lifestyle. That's the privilege of membership in the Reserve Cellar Wine Club. It includes a number of exclusive benefits and opportunities, like discounted wine prices, exclusive access to the Villa San-Juliette property, and priority pricing and event tickets. The Reserve Cellar is completely free to join.

A trip to Villa San-Juliette shows that the picturesque wine destination embraces leisure and embodies craftsmanship, all while providing unforgettable estate-grown Bordeaux-style and Rhône-style wines. The artisan foods and breathtaking views are pretty impressive, too.

TOP: The winemaking at Villa San-Juliette is meticulous and detail-oriented, ensuring the highest quality of its estate wines.
Photograph by Gracie Warwick

RIGHT: Up-and-coming winemaker Dan Smith sips a glass of his distinguished Chorum red blend.
Photograph by Brandon Stier

Vina Robles Vineyards & Winery   PASO ROBLES

Growers and makers of expressive, approachable Paso Robles estate wines, Vina Robles owners Hans Nef and Hans -R. Michel began farming wine grapes in 1997. It was a mere 30 years after the region's first Cabernet Sauvignon was planted by Dr. Stanley Hoffman and the legendary André Tchelistcheff. Entrepreneurs who would later become known as pioneers of the region followed; they experimented and made discoveries that would shape the future of the Paso Robles wine industry. This land and this spirit are what drew Nef and Michel to the region, and inspired them to purchase property that would become their first of six Paso Robles estate vineyards.

The 40-plus wineries that existed in 1997 have grown in number to more than 200. It is now no secret that growing conditions in Paso Robles are optimal for producing premium and ultra-premium wines. By 2012, Nef and Michel recognized how the diversity of terroir within the region contributed to nuances in fruit grown in different areas. They took up a petition with a few like-minded vineyard owners and ultimately helped to establish 11 sub-AVAs/ districts in 2014.

FACING PAGE: Dotted with signature Paso Robles oaks, the Vina Robles estate Huerhuero Vineyard straddles the borderline of the El Pomar and Geneseo Districts.

ABOVE: Guests are welcomed by a lush arbor at the Vina Robles Hospitality Center.
Photographs by Barry Goyette

The Vina Robles vineyard team currently farms a total of 2,400 acres on six estate vineyards, all are SIP Certified Sustainable. Only the finest blocks from each site are farmed for Vina Robles wines, the balance is sold to other area wineries. Spread out over the region, these six vineyards represent five of Paso's 11 sub-AVAs.

125

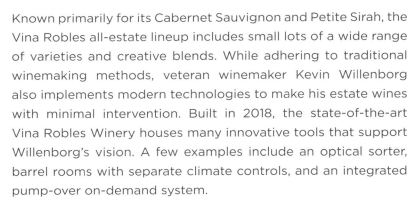

Known primarily for its Cabernet Sauvignon and Petite Sirah, the Vina Robles all-estate lineup includes small lots of a wide range of varieties and creative blends. While adhering to traditional winemaking methods, veteran winemaker Kevin Willenborg also implements modern technologies to make his estate wines with minimal intervention. Built in 2018, the state-of-the-art Vina Robles Winery houses many innovative tools that support Willenborg's vision. A few examples include an optical sorter, barrel rooms with separate climate controls, and an integrated pump-over on-demand system.

Willenborg came to Vina Robles in 2012. Versatile and detail-oriented, he brings more than 30 years of winemaking experience, covering many of the industry's key regions including Bordeaux, Napa, Sonoma and British Columbia's Okanagan Valley as well as California's Central Coast. His team approach and passion for "winegrowing" allows him to craft elegant wines that are truly expressive of the Vina Robles estate vineyards.

TOP: At the inviting Tasting Room, first-class hospitality is offered by way of unique, memorable experiences with wine, food, and music at their core.

BELOW LEFT: Longtime friends and business associates, Vina Robles owners Hans Nef and Hans -R. Michel have been growing Paso Robles wine grapes since 1997.

BELOW RIGHT: The beautiful Vina Robles fountain stands at the center of the Jardine Court, where guests can enjoy wine tasting, bistro service, and live music.
Photographs by Barry Goyette

CABERNET SAUVIGNON

GOURMET PAIRINGS

The cassis and blueberry flavors in the Vina Robles Cabernet Sauvignon lend themselves beautifully to a grilled, smoky steak. For an even more satisfying experience, add a sauce made with dried cherries.

TASTING NOTES

This garnet Cabernet Sauvignon has an aroma of cassis, blueberry, cedar, and anise, with hints of black olives and juniper berry. It is full-bodied with licorice notes and chewy, and chalky tannins. The fruit for this wine was selected from two of the estate vineyards in Paso Robles—Huerhuero and Creston Valley. Both produce Cabernet Sauvignon with an overall balance of expressive flavors and structure.

WINEMAKER'S INSIGHT

All the blocks were handpicked and sorted in the early morning to ensure quality and uniformity of ripeness. Then the fruit was destemmed and gently crushed into temperature-controlled stainless-steel tanks. Pump-overs took place regularly to enhance color and help extract tannins from the skin. After pressing, the wine was racked into barrels to complete malolactic fermentation.

AWARDS & DISTINCTIONS

95 points, Gold Medal, Best of Class – Los Angeles International Wine Competition
92 points – Editors' Choice, *Wine Enthusiast*
91 points – Tasting Panel
Double Gold – Central Coast Wine Competition

TECHNICAL DATA

APPELLATION: Paso Robles
COMPOSITION: 84% Cabernet Sauvignon, 16% Petit Verdot
MATURATION: The wine is aged 20 months in French, Hungarian, and American oak barrels.
CELLARING: Ages beautifully for 20-plus years, yet enticing to drink on release.

ORDER OUR WINE

Visit website by scanning the image to left

Windward Vineyard PASO ROBLES

Marc Goldberg and Maggie D'Ambrosia have an intense passion for Pinot Noir. For the owners and winemakers of Windward Vineyard, the passion runs so deep that they have produced this varietal exclusively for the past 25 years in the distinctive Burgundian style.

Goldberg was bitten by the Pinot Noir bug on his travels to Burgundy. His vision was to make a "great American, Burgundian style wine," as he states. Marc and Maggie, former hospital administrators, searched locations on the Central Coast that would support their vision.

In 1989, the couple found a 26-acre barley farm that came with a 70-year-old barn in an enclave on Paso's west side. The region, blessed with cool ocean breezes blowing through the Templeton Gap plus the calcareous soils, proved to be ideal for Pinot Noir. The 15-acre vineyard was planted in 1990 and the first vintage was produced in 1993.

The majority of grapes grown in Paso at the time were mainly sent to Napa, and Goldberg was advised by local growers that the region was too hot for Pinot Noir. He soon learned the history of Pinot Noir planted in Paso Robles by Dr. Stanley Hoffman in the mid 1960s, under the advice of the famous wine consultant, Andre Tchelistcheff, who recommended Pinot Noir planting in this microclimate. When Goldberg happened to taste Hoffman's 1976 vintage, he was convinced that the westside of Paso was ideal for Pinot Noir.

FACING PAGE: The tasting room of Windward Vineyard was established in 1989.

ABOVE: Husband and wife owners Maggie D'Ambrosia and Marc Goldberg enjoy the fruits of their labor over a wine barrel at Windward Vineyard.
Photographs courtesy of Windward Vineyard

Since the winery offers just one varietal, visitors experience a vertical tasting of four vintages. A bonus tasting includes Vin Gris de Pinot Noir, a rosé fragrant with strawberry aromas and a unique white-rosé hybrid produced from 100 percent estate Pinot Noir grapes.

Windward is proud of its many awards including Double Gold for both its 2013 and 2014 vintages from the San Francisco Chronicle Wine Competition. The signature profile of a Windward Pinot Noir is one of balance—with aromas of violets and ripe bing cherry layered with traces of earthy notes.

At Windward, it's a family affair. On most days you will find Marc and Maggie or their son, Justin in the tasting room. The scenic terrace is an ideal place for a glass of wine enjoyed with a selection of charcuterie and cheeses available.

TOP LEFT: Guests enjoy the patio overlooking our 15-acre vineyard. It's a perfect place for a picnic.
Photograph courtesy of Windward Vineyard

TOP RIGHT: Heather, Marc, and Pinot enjoy a glass of our Pinot rosé during a special Harvest Lunch.
Photograph by Heather Goodman

LOWER LEFT: Our pups, Pinot and Porcini, pose next to a magnum of our 20th anniversary bottle. We're dog friendly, feel free to bring your four-legged friends with you.
Photograph by Heather Goodman

LOWER RIGHT: Our bocce ball court and lush patio is shaded by oak and walnut trees. You can't beat that view.
Photograph by Dina Mande, Juice Media

MONOPOLE PINOT NOIR

GOURMET PAIRINGS

Serve with wild salmon with sautéed chanterelle mushrooms and kale. The Estate Pinot Noir has layered herbal complexity that is highlighted by the mushrooms and the finesse to complement the salmon.

TASTING NOTES

This wine shows with fruit on the nose, such as fresh Bing cherries and wild strawberries followed by floral violet notes. On the palate, the balanced acidity shines with notes of caramel-wrapped cherry mingling with earthy notes of cigar box, sandalwood, and French vanilla which balances the fruit and adds to its layered complexity. The round mouthfeel with subtle tannin leads to a prolonged peacock-tail finish, reminiscent of Nuits-Saint- George and Vosne-Romanée vineyards.

WINEMAKER'S INSIGHT

This wine is crafted in much the same tried-and-true methods each year, such that each vintage truly represents the vineyard as it evolves and changes with minimal intervention. The winemaker does not fine, filter, nor acidulate the wines. The fruit is exclusively sourced from the estate vineyard in the breezy, cool Templeton Gap. Fruit is hand harvested, de-stemmed, and pressed.

AWARDS & DISTINCTIONS

Winemaker of the Year – SLO County
Wine Industry Persons of the Year
Double Gold Medal – San Francisco Chronicle Wine Competition
93 points – International Wine Review.
Gold Medal – Sommelier Challenge Int'l Wine Competition
Gold Medal – Annual Pinot Noir Shootout

TECHNICAL DATA

APPELLATION: Paso Robles, Templeton Gap
COMPOSITION: 100% Estate Pinot Noir
MATURATION: Aged in 100 percent Seguin Moreau French oak barrels, and 30 percent new, for 18 months.
CELLARING: The wines are crafted to improve with age. Vintages 15 to 20 years old still show excellent color, robust fruit profiles, and layered complexity.

ORDER OUR WINE

 Visit our website by scanning the image to left

Signature Wines and Wineries of Coastal California

Cooper-Garrod Estate Vineyards SARATOGA

The Cooper-Garrod story begins in 1893 when English immigrants, David and Sophia Garrod, purchased property above Saratoga from the Mount Eden Orchard and Vineyard Company. From then on, the Garrods were a farming family that grew their passion into what now includes 28 acres of organic vineyards. David and Sophia's granddaughter, Louise, played a pivotal role in the winery's history when she met George Cooper at UC Berkeley in the 1930s. The two married, and after WWII when George began to work as a research test pilot at NASA/Ames, they settled at the Garrod family ranch. Cooper and Garrod cousins grew up together, and when George was ready for retirement in 1972, he chose to pursue winemaking in his golden years. George planted Cabernet Sauvignon on the Garrod family estate with guidance from neighbor and legendary winemaker, Martin Ray, and help from family members. Over the next 20 years, George and his nephew, Jan Garrod, expanded the vineyards to include Chardonnay, Cabernet Franc, and additional Cabernet Sauvignon. The Cooper and Garrod families enjoyed a truly private reserve during this time, ultimately leading to establishment of a bonded winery in 1994. The premier commercial release, a 1992 Chardonnay, won the first of many prestigious awards. Today the vineyards yield about 80 tons of estate fruit per year, some sold to other wineries, and estate annual production is around 2,000 cases. Varietals now also include Viognier, Pinot Noir, Syrah, Merlot, and the Test Pilot series, which are estate blends. Cooper-Garrod is a CCOF Certified Organic Vineyard and CCSW Certified Sustainable Vineyard and Winery.

FACING PAGE: A trail ride returns home past the Gravel Ridge vineyard in this bucolic setting only 20 minutes from Silicon Valley.
Photograph by Kristian Melom

ABOVE: Fine estate wines ready for gift givingcan be enjoyed at home or on our terrace.
Photograph courtesy of Cooper-Garrod Estate Vineyards

Co-located with Garrod Farms Riding Stables, the winery is a working ranch to this day, run by family members working side by side. The Fruit House tasting room was built in 1922 to store dried prunes and apricots until they shipped to market; the 1903 antique barn houses beautiful horses who board at Garrod Farms. Jan Garrod is the Vineyard Master; and founding Winemaker George Cooper transferred his duties to son Bill, who joined his dad in 1996. Today, Bill works with Trevor Garrod, Jan's son. Cory Bosworth is the Tasting Room and Club Manager—she and Trevor are cousins, as are Jan and Bill. Cory's mother, Vicky Garrod Bosworth, heads the Riding Academy for Garrod Farms Stables.

Guests are welcome to enjoy the family's traditional California ranch hospitality and taste wine where the grapes are grown. Horseback riding is available daily along trails with panoramic views of the San Francisco Bay area. Visitors can opt for the monthly Walk with the Winemaker tour, check out the quarterly Eco-tour, or enjoy numerous seasonal festivals and events.

TOP: The Lone Oak vineyard enjoys expansive views of Silicon Valley below.
Photograph by Ralph Andrea

BELOW LEFT: Sunday "Music at the Vineyards" is a popular outing on the Cooper-Garrod patio from spring through fall.

BELOW RIGHT: Picnics are ideal at this estate vineyard and winery. Bring your own or pick up something in the tasting room.
Photographs courtesy of Cooper-Garrod Estate Vineyards

CABERNET FRANC

GOURMET PAIRINGS
Pair this wine with poultry with berry sauces, pork loin with cranberries, or lamb chops with pomegranate. Cabernet Franc is a versatile wine with nuances that complement several meats.

TASTING NOTES
Cabernet Franc pours a rich red garnet into your glass, with aromas that bring to mind a bowl of mixed berries with tantalizing brown spices. Across the palate, you will find raspberries and cherries with a pinch of cardamom, cloves, and allspice. The smooth finish is like a waterfall of juicy, red fruits.

WINEMAKER'S INSIGHT
Cooper-Garrod wines are made from estate-grown, sustainably farmed, hand-harvested organic grapes. The mountain vineyards are picked in multiple lots for ideal ripeness. Destemmed whole berries ferment in small fermenters with native yeasts. Naturally occurring malolactic fermentation completes in barrel and is followed with minimal effective sulfur. The wine is pad filtered at bottling. This minimal intervention is the sum of our actions.

AWARDS & DISTINCTIONS
Silver Medal – San Francisco Chronicle Wine Competition
90-plus points – *Wine Enthusiast*

TECHNICAL DATA

APPELLATION: Santa Cruz Mountains
COMPOSITION: 100% Estate Cabernet Franc
MATURATION: Aged 10 months in French Oak, 30 percent new.
CELLARING: It's luscious upon release, but can also be cellared a decade or more to enjoy progressive maturation.

ORDER OUR WINE

Visit our wine store by scanning the image to left

Foxen Vineyard SANTA MARIA

Nestled in the scenic terrain of northern Santa Barbara County, Foxen Vineyard and Winery is run by a team that has a couple of basic principles about wine. First, small-batch, sustainably farmed production is the best way to go. And second, vineyard-focused wines with a straightforward, minimalist approach offer the best results. Bill Wathen—a self-proclaimed vineyard guy—and Dick Doré have been making wine under that philosophy since 1985, when they founded Foxen Winery & Vineyard at the historic Rancho Tinaquaic. The pair actually made their very first wine on Dick's basketball court.

Named after Dick's great-great grandfather William Benjamin Foxen, the winery's story goes as far back as the early 1800s when he first came to the area and purchased Rancho Tinaquaic. Foxen—who was also an English sea captain—bought the land with a Mexican land grant that gave him almost 9,000 acres that is now known as Foxen Canyon. He adopted the distinctive anchor as his ranch cattle brand, which became the apt trademark for the company. Today, the winery and vineyards are made up of 2,000 acres of the land purchased by Captain Foxen.

The land also houses the winery's original tasting room, endearingly referred to as the Shack. Constructed in the late 1800s, the building was first used as a blacksmith shop for the ranch. In 1987, however, it became Dick and Bill's tasting room, which they ran for many years. With a much more modern approach, a solar-powered tasting room opened in 2009 alongside the new winery—also solar powered. It's called Foxen 7200, and its focus

FACING PAGE: Sunset view of Foxen's solar-powered winery and tasting room in Foxen Canyon.

ABOVE: Co-founders Dick Doré (left) and Bill Wathen (right) in the barrel room at Foxen Vineyard.
Photographs by Jeremy Ball

PINOT NOIR

GOURMET PAIRINGS

Pairs wonderfully with pan-seared, fresh Northwest salmon and morel mushrooms

TASTING NOTES

This beauty was brought up all in three- and four-year-old barrels. Sporting a vivid ruby/purple-tinged color as well as notes of wild strawberries, black raspberries, scorched earth, forest floor, and salty minerality, it hits the palate with medium-bodied depth and richness, vibrant acidity, and a fresh, focused core that's mostly covered by the upfront 2016 fruit. It is pure and vibrant, and while you can certainly drink this beauty today, it's going to evolve gracefully on its balance.

AWARDS & DISTINCTIONS

92 points - JebDunnuck.com
91+ points - *Wine Advocate*
91 points - *Wine Spectator*

TECHNICAL DATA

APPELLATION: Santa Maria Valley
COMPOSITION: 100% Pinot Noir
MATURATION: Aged a minimum of 24 months in oak barrels.
CELLARING: Ages beautifully for 10-plus years, yet enticing to drink on release.

ORDER OUR WINE

Visit our website by scanning the image to left

is on Bordeaux and Italian-style wines, and also showcases Burgundian and Rhône-style wines. It is surrounded by native-plant landscaping, all maintained with minimal irrigation, and sits next to the estate dry-farmed vineyard block.

Winemaker David Whitehair began his tenure at Foxen in 2007, and it's only fitting that he is a true local-born and raised in the Santa Ynez Valley. David has worked in New Zealand, as well as Chalk Hill in Healdsburg, and takes a hands-on approach to his craft. He joined the team after a chance meeting with Bill that led to his immediate hiring at Foxen. He considers his work a privilege and is honored to work under the founders. He believes that, "[Winemaking] begins with the vines and soil and ends in the glass. It's a fine balance between science and art."

TOP LEFT: Foxen 7200 tasting "shack" on Foxen Canyon Road.

TOP RIGHT: Winemaking team at Foxen (left to right): Winemaker David Whitehair and Foxen co-founder and director of farming and winemaking, Bill Wathen

ABOVE: The solar-powered winery and tasting room was completed in 2009. *Photographs by Jeremy Ball*

Sanford Winery LOMPOC

Owned and cared for by the Terlato Family, the picturesque Sanford Winery is located in the heart of the scenic Santa Rita Hills. The Sanford estate, which was once part of the original Rancho Santa Rosa land grant of 1872, is comprised of the winery itself along with two separate and distinct vineyards: the historically significant Sanford & Benedict Vineyard and the La Rinconada Vineyard.

The iconic Sanford & Benedict Vineyard is home to the first Pinot Noir vineyard in Santa Barbara County, planted in 1973 by Michael Benedict and his then partner Richard Sanford. Its unique soil composition was formed by a landslide around 6,000 to 10,000 years ago, resulting in deep, fractured, marine-based Monterey shale with very high water-holding capacity. It is the ideal land for rooted vines to thrive as they search and dive deep for hydration and nutrients. Because of this, the entire site was planted with Vitus Vinifera without being grafted to rootstocks, and subsequently dry farmed until 1994. Michael Benedict researched the entire West Coast using his viticultural climate model and selected this site specifically to grow Burgundian varieties, Pinot Noir, and Chardonnay.

La Rinconada, or "corner place," sits on the corner of the ranch and was traditionally planted in 1994 in deep alluvial soil that was deposited by the Santa Ynez River. The parcel was created as an oxbow in the meandering river during the late Pleistocene epoch, which dates as far back as 2.5 million years ago. It has also been suggested that the "corner place" references an age-old

FACING PAGE: Doors opening to reveal Sanford's magnificent woodwork and stonework in the Barrel Room.

ABOVE: Early morning fog burning off over the Sanford & Benedict Vineyard.
Photographs by Jeremy Ball

141

SANFORD PINOR NOIR, SANFORD & BENEDICT VINEYARD

GOURMET PAIRINGS

The savory nature of sous vide beef ribeye steak—featuring a quick pan sear—pairs well with the terroir while the fat of the steak balances out this structured wine.

TASTING NOTES

The Sanford & Benedict, estate grown Pinot Noir entices with aromatic spicy red fruits, complemented by notes of earth and dried herb. The palate delivers earthy raspberry flavors with lush, silky texture. The bright acidity and supple tannins give the wine great structure and length.

WINEMAKER'S INSIGHT

The iconic and historic Sanford & Benedict Vineyard contains the oldest Pinot Noir vines in Santa Barbara County. Between the history and the amazing quality of the fruit, many consider this site deserving of Grand Cru status. To allow the vineyard to shine through, the team takes a gentle approach in the cellar, using traditional Burgundian techniques that include open-top fermenters and hand-selected French oak barrels.

AWARDS & DISTINCTIONS

94 points – *Wine Enthusiast*
92 points – *Wine Spectator*
94 points – *Jeb Dunnuck*

TECHNICAL DATA

APPELLATION: Santa Rita Hills, Sanford & Benedict Vineyard
COMPOSITION: 100% Pinot Noir
MATURATION: Aged 14 months in hand-selected, French oak barrels—35 percent new.
CELLARING: The Sanford & Benedict Pinot Noir has the balance and structure to age beautifully for the next 12 to 15 years.

LEARN MORE

Visit our website by scanning image on left.

marker located in the far reaches of the ranch which denotes a corner of the original Rancho Santa Rosa land grant in the mid-1800s.

The Sanford Winery itself stands as a tribute to California Mission Architecture, utilizing sustainable building techniques and hand-crafted wine production. The winery, named for one of its founders, is built of hand-cast adobe brick and recycled Douglas fir from an early 20th century sawmill building in Washington state.

Sanford has enjoyed a renaissance under the Terlato Family's stewardship and care. John Terlato, working closely with the winemaking team, has brought to life the family's vision of unlocking the full potential of the vineyards through sustainable farming and thoughtful winemaking. Winemaker Trey Fletcher is a careful, perceptive, and experienced winemaker who is committed to crafting wines which are clear reflections of the vineyards. Laura Roach is the assistant winemaker, Erik Mallea the vineyard manager, and Auggie Rodriguez the cellar master—all who play critical roles in day-to-day operations.

The entire Sanford team shares a common vision: to craft wines which are precise, unadulterated representations of their vineyards and which fully unlock the potential of the vineyard and its varietals. This clear philosophy, to be properly executed, requires thoughtfulness and meticulous attention to 1,000 details. This begins with sustainable farming along

TOP: Each small lot of Sanford grapes are hand sorted at the winery following night harvest–here by assistant winemaker Laura Roach and owner John Terlato.

ABOVE: John takes a moment to pause and enjoy the beauty of Sanford vineyards and tasting room.

LEFT: The barrel room also serves as an intimate space for private tastings and events.
Photographs by Jeremy Ball

143

with precise and—attentive yet restrained—winemaking. John Terlato intones, "In winemaking, we are certainly involved but we must always be careful not to intercede. This approach to winemaking benefits from a winemaker who is equal parts right and left brained, possessing confidence and creativity, along with time-honed skills and experience, all of which is then applied thoughtfully and with restraint. The vision of Sanford Winery is entirely based on what our unique vineyards have to offer, and in the end, our successes are founded in our vineyards. It's all about the vineyards."

Guests are invited for daily tours and tastings and a wide variety of seasonal events and festivals. A few special options include the Valentine Barrel Room Dinner, Pinot Blending and Lobster Feast, and Eggs & Benedict Brunch. There are also more traditional harvest parties, holiday celebrations, and club release events.

TOP: Sanford Winery uses unique hydraulic equipment that rotates the wines in tanks using the natural force of gravity for selected wines.

ABOVE The iconic original Sanford & Benedict barn gets its striking color from natural moss, no paint required.
Photographs by Jeremy Ball

SANFORD PINOT NOIR, SANTA RITA HILLS

GOURMET PAIRINGS

The bright red fruit flavors of our Sta. Rita Hills Pinot Noir pair beautifully with herb-crusted leg of lamb. The fruit, earth, and savory notes balance the richness of the lamb perfectly.

TASTING NOTES

The Santa Rita Hills estate-grown Pinot Noir is bright, red ruby in color and is bursting with black raspberry and orange peel, along with savory notes of lavender and white pepper. The palate delivers dense dusty, berry flavors with balanced acid and tannin structure, which carries on with a long and lovely finish.

WINEMAKER'S INSIGHT

The Santa Rita Hills Pinot Noir is a blend of fruit from two estate vineyards: the historic and iconic Sanford & Benedict Vineyard and La Rinconada Vineyard. A range of Pinot clones and soil types provide the winemakers with all the components to make beautiful wines from vintage to vintage. Classic Burgundian cellar techniques were employed in making this wine, including open-top fermentation and aging in French oak barrels.

AWARDS & DISTINCTIONS

93 points – *Wine Enthusiast*
90 points – *Jeb Dunnuck*
90 points – *Wine Spectator*

TECHNICAL DATA

APPELLATION: Santa Rita Hills
COMPOSITION: 100% Pinot Noir
MATURATION: Aged 10 months in French oak barrels—30 percent new.
CELLARING: Delicious upon release, the Santa Rita Hills Pinot Noir will cellar beautifully for up to 10 years.

ORDER OUR WINE

Visit our wine store by scanning the image to left

Vincent Vineyards & Winery SANTA YNEZ

Vincent Vineyards was established in 2007 and embraces an Old-World theme with a love for Bordeaux wine. The winery's name has two significant meanings. First, Vincent is the middle name of the establishment's patriarch, Tony Vincent Zehenni, who often uses Vincent as his last name. Second, Saint Vincent is the official patron saint of winemakers. The feast of Saint Vincent is celebrated every year on January 22, which is ideal for winegrowers as it symbolizes a midpoint in the vine's growing cycle.

Tony and Tanya Vincent operate the family-owned winery, and the staff embraces the founder's tradition of quality and excellence. Vincent Vineyards commits itself daily to the farming, winemaking, and customer experience requisite to its quality estate wines. While visiting Santa Ynez, Tony and Tanya fell in love with the undeniably charming area. They were looking for a new adventure and decided to transform their passion for wine and hospitality into the family business. The Vincents visited stunning wineries around the world and were especially inspired by the French process of winemaking. Their vines were imported from France and cultivated in the U.S. before they were planted in Santa Ynez.

The estate-grown wines are primarily Bordeaux varietals, although they do offer Rhônes such as a Syrah, which won a gold medal in the first year of production. Their award-winning Sauvignon-Blanc, Rosé and Rosé sparkling wines are white wine lovers' favorites. And in keeping with the annual tradition of new reveals, they will introduce a Port in the fall. Those familiar with the region know Santa Ynez is climatically ideal for wine growing–particularly the

FACING PAGE: The oval, handcrafted walnut bar with the marble top is centered to view the outdoor patio and breathtaking view of the vineyard.

ABOVE: The view of the entrance to Vincent Vineyards & Winery in Santa Ynez.
Photographs by David Lillich Photography

Cabernet grape. To create the type, style, and tecture of wines desired, Vincent Vineyards & Winery understands the delicate balance of farming, cultivation, stock, and soil necessary to produce top-quality wines. Their focus on creating exceptional wines beginswith a specialized approach to conditioning the soil as they know every element of the process is essential and ends with their outstanding winemaker's magic touch.

The Vincent Winery provides guests with a high-quality experience by offering exclusive wines in an exceptional atmosphere. Whether in the tasting room or along the vineyard terrace, guests enjoy exquisite views of the vineyard-covered estate along with one of the more majestic mountain vistas that the valley has to offer. It's one of the few wineries in Santa Ynez where you can sit and enjoy table service while wine tasting. Vincent Winery's attentive staff will share the story of each wine, the winemaking style, and the Vincent family history. The wines are not available for wholesale or retail purchase, so as a boutique vineyard, the small-case lot production can only be experienced at the Vincent estate and select restaurants.

TOP: A classic 1950 Packard Woody in front of the vineyard adds to the breathtaking views of the property.

BELOW LEFT: The Vincent barrel room has all the equipment which produce our estate wine. The premium French barrels craft a unique barrel tasting experience for the Vincent Vineyards guests.

BELOW RIGHT: Harvest season is a time of cultivation of our estate wines. Our grapes are delicately harvested by hand.
Photographs by David Lillich Photography

CABERNET SAUVIGNON

GOURMET PAIRINGS
Pairs wonderfully beef and lamb.

TASTING NOTES

The Vincent Vineyards Cabernet Sauvignon features complex characters of raspberry, cranberry, blackberry, and red currants with undertones of tobacco and minerals. Notes of toasted marshmallow, cedar, and vanilla dance on your tongue. Beautifully refined tannins accent an elegant structure and a long, distinguished finish.

WINEMAKER'S INSIGHT

The Cabernet Sauvignon lots were all hand-sorted then destemmed and cold-soaked for three days. The grapes were then fermented in closed-top fermenters and pumped over twice a day. The wine was then pressed off the skins and racked to French barrels—30 percent new oak. After aging for 22 months in the barrel, the four lots of Cabernet Sauvignon are racked together and blended for bottling.

AWARDS & DISTINCTIONS

Bronze Medal – Orange County Wine Society
Double Gold, Best of Class – LA International Wine Competition
97 points, Gold Medal – LA International Wine Competition
90 points, Silver Medal – California State Fair Sacramento,

TECHNICAL DATA

APPELLATION: Santa Ynez Valley
COMPOSITION: 100% Estate Cabernet Sauvignon, alcohol 14.2%
MATURATION: Aged 22 months in new French oak.
CELLARING: Enjoy now or cellar for up to 20 years.

ORDER OUR WINE

Visit our website by scanning the image to left

DeTierra Vineyards, page 191

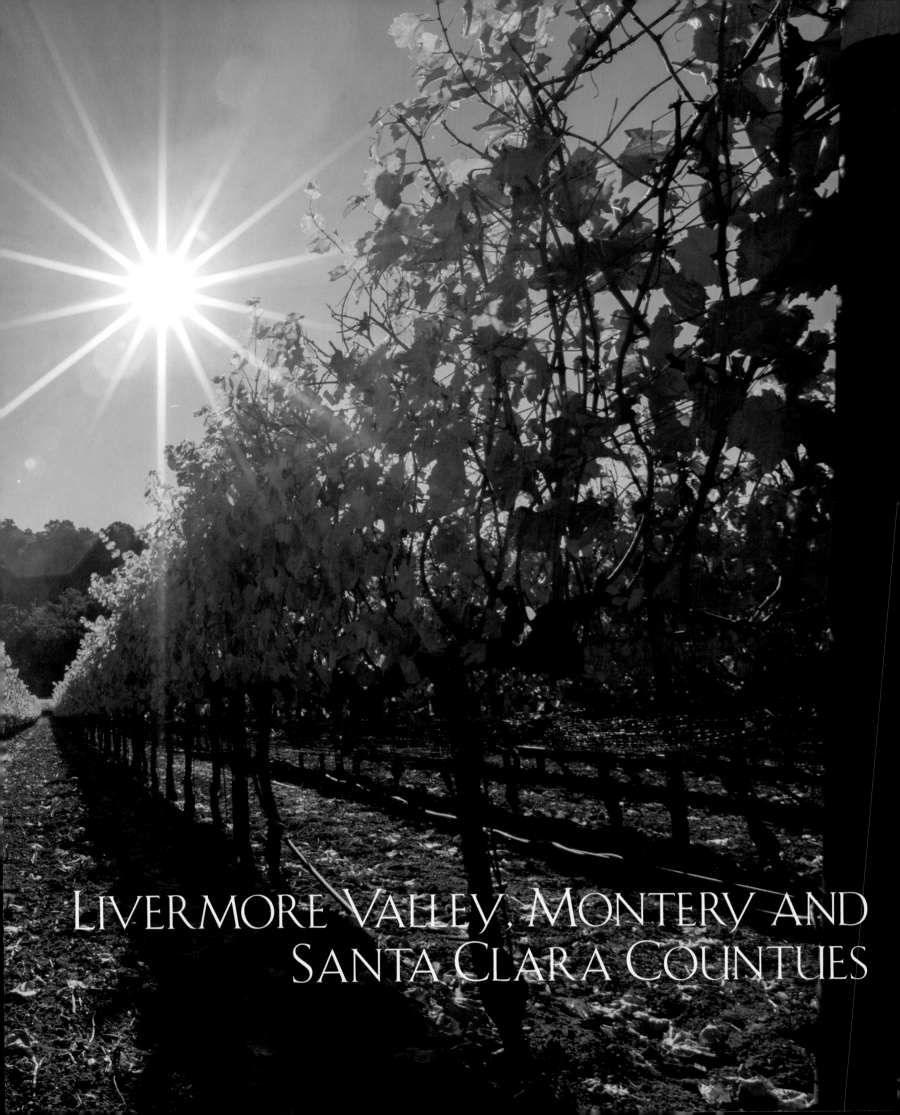

LIVERMORE VALLEY, MONTERY AND
SANTA CLARA COUNTUES

Big White House Winery
John Evan Cellars

LIVERMORE VALLEY

Although it may seem odd for a three-year-old to choose the name for a California winery, it makes perfect sense when you hear the story of Winemaker John Evan Marion.

John witnessed the winemaking process from an early age, and grew up with wine being made in his backyard. His parents, John the Elder and Diana, moved the family from a small tract home into a high-ceiling, white, Colonial Revival-style house when he was just a toddler. And as you may have guessed, young John Evan deemed it "the big white house." Years later, when the winemaking began, the adults liked the sound of it and labeled the wine as such—and the name has stuck ever since.

John picked up winemaking as a hobby and started officially getting his hands dirty at the ripe age of 15. He got the chance to sample vintages on trips to Paris even earlier. John went commercial in 1998 and has been honing his craft over the last few decades. In the early days, he had to distinguish his work from his father's, hence the name John Evan Cellars. At family gatherings, his father John II, (now Winemaker Emeritus) was referred to as Johnny, while the young winemaker, John III, was known as John Evan. As the years passed, John's friends entered into the corporate world and began to express dissatisfaction with work life, which made John even more certain he had found his calling. He fell in love with the art, labor, long hours, and what felt like magic, of the enological life.

FACING PAGE: The little barn turned winery features doors made from century-old, redwood wine tanks and stunning sunset-soaked vineyard views.

ABOVE The rustic yet refined aesthetic welcomes you into the homey tasting room.
Photographs by Adam J Clark

JOHN EVAN CELLARS
THE TALKING BULL

GOURMET PAIRINGS

Pair with The Talking Bull almost any meat or game. The winery team's particular favorite is an oak-smoked Muscovy duck with black currant and thyme coulis. A close second would be a seared rib-eye with Roquefort compound butter.

TASTING NOTES

Ink-black in color, The Talking Bull showcases black cherry, plum, black tea, and pie spice in the nose. The flavors mirror the nose and, while many Petite Sirahs are pure drying tannin in the mouth, The Talking Bull reveals bold tannins but is balanced by excellent acidity and a long, lingering finish.

WINEMAKER'S INSIGHT

This flagship wine comes from a one-acre, head-trained vineyard that produces a mere two-and-a-half tons of grapes every year. Petite Sirah is a variety that grows exceptionally well in Livermore Valley and this particular vineyard produces some of the best fruit in the area. Mimicking the personality of Jay, the owner of this vineyard, The Talking Bull is the perfect mixture of confidence, eloquence, charm, and elegance in the glass.

TECHNICAL DATA

APPELLATION: Livermore Valley
COMPOSITION: 100% Petite Sirah
MATURATION: Aged 33 to 35 months in French oak barrels.
CELLARING: Beautifully open and balanced upon release, this wine has the structure to age well for 20 years or more.

LEARN MORE

Visit our website by scanning the image on the left

Set in the close-knit wine community of Livermore Valley, the winery's tasting room is a charming converted barn that is big on personality. Far from the tailored, grandiose wineries in other regions, Big White House and John Evan offer a comfortable—and educational—approach to wine. Guests are encouraged to belly up to the bar with their lists of questions for the staff. From the technical to the philosophical, inquiries come in all forms, and the Big White House team members (who consider themselves ever-evolving students of the process) embrace the opportunity to share insight and knowledge.

The tasting room's artwork is hard to miss upon entering, with roughly 40 images adorning the walls. Striking and lively, the works are made by John's sister, Laura Marion. The art changes and rotates, showing off wine labels from past and present vintages. Oftentimes, the featured art reveals what is being sampled at the bar.

TOP: The spectacular Petite Sirah from the head-trained Davis-King Vineyard is made into The Talking Bull.
Photograph by Fenton Kremer

BELOW LEFT: The patio has a gorgeous vineyard vista. It's a fantastic spot for a picnic.
Photograph by Adam J Clark

BELOW RIGHT: Winemaker John Evan Marion examines the newly set grape crop that will become The Talking Bull with his son, John IV.
Photograph by Fenton Kremer

In addition to the Marion family, including John's wife and son, the winery team includes Jessica Carroll as Assistant Winemaker, and Stephanie Rebiejo as Vice President and Club Manager. The staff has an obvious passion for what they do and do an excellent job of conveying the magic and hard work that goes into every aspect of their craft. Priding themselves on the use of traditional methods, the winemakers use minimal intervention and yet, with methods such as co-fermentation, still practice innovation.

Varietals change from year to year, but a few that always make the cut include Petite Sirah, Syrah, Cabernet Sauvignon, and Sangiovese. Obscure varietals are a specialty at Big White House and John Evan, so if you're into that, keep an eye out for upcoming features; they change every few years.

TOP: In the open tasting room you'll find dozens of paintings by the resident artist, Laura Marion.

BELOW LEFT: Look for Big White House Winery and John Evan Cellars at the end of the beautiful country drive down Greenville Road. *Photographs by Adam J Clark*

BELOW RIGHT: Fun times with family are easy to find at the winery. *Photograph by Fenton Kremer*

BIG WHITE HOUSE
ALFIE'S AMALGAMATION

GOURMET PAIRINGS

Serve this with a rack of lamb with cherry demi-glace, over potatoes roasted in the same pan. Add a grilled kale salad with Satsuma-yuzu dressing to round it out.

TASTING NOTES

In the nose you'll find cinnamon, black tea, and white pepper. Good balance accentuates a mouth of bright cherry, cocoa, and allspice. You'll notice structure from the Petite Sirah, spice from the Zinfandel, and fruit from the Cabernet.

WINEMAKER'S INSIGHT

Named after the winery dog, St. Alphonso of Pancake Breakfasts, Alfie's Amalgamation is a blend of Petite Sirah, Cabernet Sauvignon, and Zinfandel—considered some of Livermore Valley's best-growing grapes. Alfie's heritage is unknown and as such, the proportions of his wine vary from year to year. Like its namesake, Alfie's Amalgamation just wants a little attention and it will reward you with love.

TECHNICAL DATA

APPELLATION: Livermore Valley
COMPOSITION: Petite Sirah, Cabernet Sauvignon, and Zinfandel, with varying proportions each vintage
MATURATION: Aged 24 months in French oak.
CELLARING: Excellent on release or can be aged up to five years in the bottle.

ORDER OUR WINE

Visit our website by scanning the image on the left.

Cuda Ridge Wines LIVERMORE VALLEY

Cuda Ridge Wines was inspired from a love affair—with a car. A 1970 plum crazy purple Barracuda, to be exact. In the 1990s, Larry and Margie Dino were looking to buy some property in Sonoma. The couple took a long, frustrating drive to see the property but the land had a nonnegotiable price. The Dinos passed on the purchase, but as they were driving home, Larry saw the car of his dreams for sale on the side of the road. If he couldn't have the land he wanted, he would at least have the car. Larry made a hefty investment and spent the next three years having the car restored. Margie called the car his mistress because it stole so much time, attention, and passion from her husband.

The year was 1999 and the couple was making wine in their garage, with the barrel next to the car. Margie said the wine took on the subtle aroma and taste of the car. So, when they had a bottling party and were trying to come up with a name for our first home vintage, Larry's car-enthusiast friend naturally proposed the idea of Cuda Ridge Wines. The couple loved the reference to their purple beauty and the name stuck. Today, the wine label is the color of the car, and if you look closely, the ridge on the label is a subliminal drawing of the car.

In 2003, the Dinos moved to Livermore, planted a small vineyard, and built a barrel room in the garage. With the home vineyard, and a controlled environment for storing, the wine became impressive. Four years later, they rented a humble building on a friend's land in a rural area of Livermore, and they got all the state and federal licensing and bonding to start producing

FACING PAGE: Proprietors Larry and Margie Dino in front of Cuda Ridge Wines.

ABOVE: Side photograph of the winery looking from the vineyard.
Photographs by Frank Anzalone

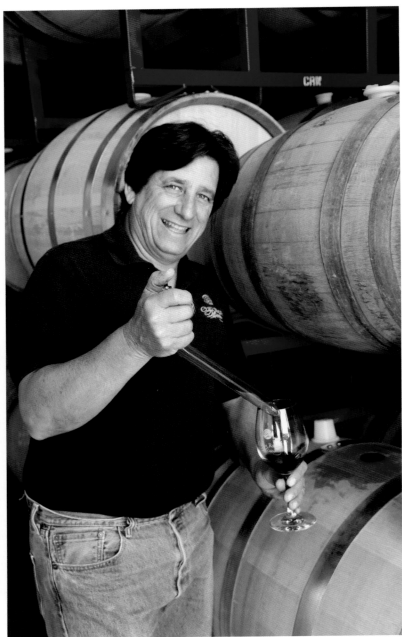

commercial wine. Larry had developed a passion for Old World, Bordeaux-style wines, which would later become some of the region's best. The first commercial harvest was in 2007, and the couple started selling wine in 2008. Initial varietals were Cabernet Sauvignon, Merlot, and Cabernet Franc. Because Cabernet Franc was not a widely produced varietal in Livermore at the time, and it was a nice wine, it soon became a signature varietal of Cuda Ridge Wines. Over the next few years, they expanded offerings to include Petit Verdot and Malbec, which have become regional favorites, as well. They rounded out the lineup with the Bordeaux whites, Sauvignon Blanc, and Semillon.

Cuda Ridge consistently wins high awards at the San Francisco Wine Competition, Orange County Fair, and local competitions. It has also received numerous 90-plus-point ratings from *Wine Enthusiast*. You can sample these for yourself at the winery and tasting room, located in a beautiful wine country setting on Arroyo Road overlooking the vineyards and hillsides.

TOP LEFT: Cuda Ridge Wines Tasting Room

BELOW LEFT: Purple label wines are considered Bordeaux-style wines, Black label wines are non-Bordeaux. In the photo we have Cabernet Franc, Syrah, and Malbec.

ABOVE: Larry Dino, winemaker, sampling wine from the barrel.
Photographs by JFrank Anzalone

CABERNET FRANC

GOURMET PAIRINGS

This wine goes well with buttery, white fish, such as baked filet of sea bass drizzled with sweet and spicy Peking sauce.

TASTING NOTES

Cuda Ridge Wines' Cabernet Franc is soft and elegant, reminiscent of a Loire Valley Cabernet Franc. This blend, typically with Cabernet Sauvignon and Merlot, is enticingly fragrant, and has evolving flavors of raspberry, ripe cherries, white pepper, and sandlewood, with a hint of olives and vanilla. The tannins are soft which makes this a great wine to pair with food or enjoy by itself with family and friends.

WINEMAKER'S INSIGHT

This wine is sourced from the White Cat Vineyard located in the eastern side of Livermore. It is located in the rolling foothills that are sunny from morning until dusk with moderate winds in the afternoon. The long sunny days bring the fruit to ripeness and the cooling effect of the afternoon winds maintains the acidity. It produces a lighter-style Cabernet Franc, which Larry prefers. The grapes are harvested early in the morning and immediately processed.

AWARDS & DISTINCTIONS

90 points – *Wine Enthusiast*
Gold and Silver Medal – San Francisco Chronicle Wine Competition and Orange County Fair

TECHNICAL DATA

APPELLATION: Livermore Valley
COMPOSITION: More than 90 percent Cabernet Franc and blended with Cabernet Sauvignon and Merlot. Some vintages may contain low percentages of Malbec or Petit Verdot.
MATURATION: The wine is aged 18 months in French oak—40 percent new, 40 percent once-used, and 20 percent neutral.
CELLARING: It is best to cellar for seven to 10 years or longer.

ORDER OUR WINE

Visit our website by scanning the image to left

Dante Robere Vineyards LIVERMORE VALLEY

After 30-plus years of friendship, most people have some great stories to tell and a strong bond to show for it. In the case of Dan Rosenberg and Bob Bossi, they also have a winery. In 2003, Dan moved to Livermore and together, the two started traveling through California's best wine regions, tasting and exploring. They quickly discovered a preference for smaller, family-run wineries, which had an approachable, feel-good vibe that resonated with the pair—and gave them an inspiration for their future project.

In 2007, Dan and Bob began volunteering and helping a few Livermore Valley winemakers in an effort to learn the winemaking processes. The pair dreamt of turning their hobby and passion for wine and winemaking into a second career—Bob was an accountant and Dan an insurance agent. They had planted a small Zinfandel vineyard in Dan's backyard and were making wine at home. In 2012, with the support of their wives, Debbie Bossi and Ann Marie Rosenberg, the pair decided to build a new winery from the ground up. They found the perfect spot across the street from Sycamore Grove Park and purchased the adjoining six-acre Syrah vineyard, and so, Dante Robere began.

Their goal was simple: to make great wine. They've accomplished that with varietals that include Syrah, Cabernet Sauvignon, Petite Sirah, Zinfandel, Chardonnay, Sauvignon Blanc, Tempranillo, Grenache, Mourvedre, Touriga, Barbera, Carignane, Petit Verdot, and Cabernet Franc. Additionally, they make upwards of seven blends from those varietals. The philosophy is to let the grapes speak for themselves.

FACING PAGE: View of Dante Robere Vineyards winery's front entrance, peeking through early spring Syrah vineyards.

ABOVE: Arial view of Dante Robere Vineyards winery, surrounding Syrah vineyards and the foothills of the beautiful Livermore Valley.
Photographs by Ron Essex Photography

163

ESTATE RESERVE SYRAH

GOURMET PAIRING

Serve with grilled lamb chops marinated in olive oil, garlic, crushed anchovies, fresh mint, and rosemary. This Syrah makes a natural match for the intensity of grilled lamb.

TASTING NOTES

The Estate Reserve Syrah has oaky aromas and heavy, sweet-seeming oak flavors that take the forefront in this rich, full-bodied and extremely spicy wine. It shows chocolate, vanilla, nutmeg, cinnamon, ripe boysenberry, cardamom, and cedar notes coupled with a smooth, long finish.

WINEMAKER'S INSIGHT

Dante Robere owns and manages a six-and-a-half-acre Syrah vineyard. For all other varietals produced, grapes from various local growers are sourced. The team manages the Syrah vineyard to extract Syrah's varietal characteristics, and manages yields to meet production requirements while achieving a high-quality crop. They implement fermentation techniques to help bring out the essence of each of the varietals. Red wines ferment in small open containers while whites are fermented in stainless steel tanks.

AWARDS & DISTINCTIONS

89 points – *Wine Enthusiast*

TECHNICAL DATA

APPELLATION: Livermore Valley
COMPOSITION: 100% Estate Syrah
MATURATION: Aged 22 months in new French Oak.
CELLARING: The wine can be consumed now but the flavors will develop greater intensity with three to five years of aging.

ORDER OUR WINE

Visit our website by scanning the image on the left

Guests are welcome to visit the winery year-round. It offers a clean, contemporary feel with rustic finishes. The main tasting room is the heart of the space, anchored by a beautifully finished tasting bar, flanked on both sides by outdoor patios. One patio is for wine club members only, while the other, the Main Patio, features panoramic vineyard and rural views. It's an ideal spot to relax, sip a glass of wine—or a bottle—and enjoy a picnic. The most appealing aspect of the tasting room, however, is the fact that there is always a winemaker/owner available to visit with guests.

Festivals and events are always happening. Visitors can check out Barrel Tasting Weekend, Holidays in the Vineyard, Wine and Wags, Taste our Terroir, and the Harvest Festival. But you don't have to wait for a special occasion to stop by—they'll be happy to see you any time.

TOP LEFT: The tasting bar of Dante Robere Vineyards, the heart of the winery's spacious tasting room.

TOP RIGHT: The main patio of Dante Robere Vineyards tasting room in Livermore Valley with panoramic rural views of vineyards, mountains and Sycamore Grove Park.

BELOW LEFT: The winemakers pictured in their tasting room. Unique to our tasting experience is access to our winemakers, Dan (on right) and Bob (on left)-a.k.a. Dante and Robere-both love to share their winemaking experience with visitors.

BELOW RIGHT: Dante Robere Vineyards' private tasting room seats up to 10 guests for a private seated tasting and cheese pairing, guided by one of our winemakers.
Photographs by Ron Essex Photography

Longevity Wines LIVERMORE VALLEY

Started in 2004, Longevity Wines has a central theme that runs throughout the company: love. The most recognizable sign of this is the mosaic heart that appears on the wine label, but the symbol has a bigger meaning beyond its simple beauty. Started by husband and wife team Phil and Debra Long, the winery used the label as a reminder of how it all began. When Phil and Debra first started dating, he gave her an artisan glass heart for Valentine's Day. The tradition stuck and over the years, her collection grew to include stone hearts, heart planters—anything and everything heart-shaped. If you look at the label closely, you'll see the small heart shapes along with grape leaves, vines, and grape clusters. It's a perfect representation of the couple.

The pair began making wine in their garage as a hobby while they both had full-time careers. But their true love was making wine together, and they knew that's where their future was. They soon acquired a wholesale-distributor license and launched the Longevity Wine Club, an online-based wine club featuring wines from different appellations in California each month. They were on the road every weekend for months, and the club grew. They realized the current licenses allowed them to make wine under the Longevity label in other wineries, which is precisely what they began to do. The new wines were integrated into the wine club, and so the brand was launched. In July of 2008, the couple opened their own location as the first urban-style winery in the Livermore Valley. With so much stacked against them—including a recession, a serious wine-barrel injury, and an unfortunate spot across the street from a sewage plant—Debra and Phil's passion endured. Set in an ideal growing region, they expanded the winery and moved to a new location where the new winery quickly gained a few neighbors. Four wineries moved into the

FACING PAGE: Our Iconic Barn in the tasting area of our exclusive Barrel Room.

ABOVE: Our staff awaits to welcome you *(left to right)*: Shiena Avila, Tim Parsons, PressTon Boo Bear Long, Phil Long, Serra Smith, Phil Long Jr. and Susan Slater.
Photographs by Phil Long

PHIL-OSOPHY, VINTNER SELECT

GOURMET PAIRINGS
Pair with braised beef short ribs, fork-tender and served with low country grits, fried carrots, and a smoked molasses glaze.

TASTING NOTES
This "phil-osophy" is one of three signature blends. It first exhibits bright ruby red color with opaque density, then leads to a wonderful array of aromas. Complex and concentrated, the blend displays aromas of sweet black currant jam, with hints of black cherry, smoke, and flowers. Aged in French oak for 32 months, this structured, full-bodied, and opulently textured wine is thick, rich, and youthful.

WINEMAKER'S INSIGHT
For this wine, Phil decided to move toward a more traditional California Bordeaux blend. Cabernet Sauvignon is the dominant grape while the other varietals play a supporting role. In fact, the Cabernet used in this blend was awarded best of class in a San Francisco Chronicle Wine Competition.

AWARDS & DISTINCTIONS
Silver Medal – Orange County Fair Commercial Wine Competition
Silver Medal – California State Fair Commercial Wine Competition
Best of Class, Best of Region
Silver Medal – Riverside International Wine Competition
Bronze Medal – Alameda County Fair Commercial Wine Competition

TECHNICAL DATA

APPELLATION: Livermore Valley
COMPOSITION: 85% Cabernet Sauvignon, 7% Cabernet Franc, 5% Merlot, and 3% Petit Verdot
MATURATION: Aged 32 months in French Oak, and 20 percent new.
CELLARING: The 2011 classic will reward you handsomely with a bit of cellaring, yet it is drinkable and approachable now.

LEARN MORE

Visit our website by scanning the image on the left.

same building, plus two that previously existed, and one popped up across the street, plus a distillery and a brewery opened nearby. Collectively, they're known as The Block East End and make for an ideal weekend of sampling and tasting.

Phil is always ready to show visitors around and welcomes everyone to the comfortable tasting room. Although Phil is the founder and winemaker—and also serves as the vice president for the Association of African American Winemakers—he has a supportive crew that helps make it all happen. Phil Long Jr. is the assistant winemaker, Tim Parsons is general manager, Shiena Avila is the tasting room manager, and Eileen Sauer is the wine educator. The team exemplifies the same love of wine as the founders.

Debra Long passed away in 2019 but will forever remain the face of Longevity and the passion behind the wines.

TOP LEFT: Many different wines to taste and many smiles are shared daily on the patio of our Livermore tasting room.

TOP RIGHT: A customer enjoys wine and the company of Eileen and Makena in our front tasting bar.

BELOW LEFT: A close up of our award-winning wines and medals including just a sampling of our food pairing awards.

BELOW RIGHT: PressTon in the tasting room next to a bottle of his namesake wine, which is aptly named "PressTon." it is a Bordeaux blend that is always on the menu.
Photographs by Phil & Debra Long

Murrieta's Well LIVERMORE VALLEY

Murrieta's Well is nestled in the scenic countryside of the Livermore Valley and is one of California's original wine estates, with roots dating back to its establishment in the 1880s. The land is special and over the years has repeatedly caught the attention of a few important visionaries, the first of which is the winery's namesake. Joaquin Murrieta was a good Samaritan who traveled up to California from Mexico, making a name for himself along the way. As legend goes, he found the artesian well on what is now the winery estate and claimed it was the best water he had tasted along his journey. Today the well is featured as a reminder of the traveler's claim.

Louis Mel and his wife purchased the property in 1884 and used cuttings from renowned French estates Chateau d'Yquem and Chateau Margaux. Descendants of those original vines produce some of the estate's current wines, which visitors can taste at the tasting room, originally a gravity-flow winery built by Mel. While the Wente family farmed the estate since it was established, it wasn't until 1940 that Ernest Wente purchased the land; it remains in the family to this day. Fourth generation winegrower Philip Wente and acclaimed winemaker Sergio Traverso opened Murrieta's Well in 1990, naming it after the man who first discovered the special estate.

Robbie Meyer is the name behind the modern magic at Murrieta's Well and creates a portfolio of wine that lives up to the estate's rich history and standards. You are invited to sample these wines in a number of ways—all

FACING PAGE: The original gravity flow winery was converted to a tasting room when Murrieta's Well was established in 1990.
Photograph courtesy of Murrieta's Well

ABOVE: Aerial view of the winery and the original estate purchased by Louis Mel in 1884.
Photograph by Ron Essex

fun and enticing. Opt for the Wine & Food Experience and get a tour of the estate, glass in hand, followed by a seated tasting in the historic barrel room. Or you can choose The Tasting Bar: a sampling experience set up in a small-group format. Both options have a wine ambassador to guide visitors through the process. Seated tastings are available in the historic barrel room and picturesque outdoor patio.

Club members get exclusive wine and experience discounts and complimentary tastings, as well as access to exclusive member-only events and experiences. Members also have exclusive access to the Club Lounge—a space created for the community of oenophiles to sip their wine while surrounded by sweeping vineyard views.

TOP: The Murrieta's Well park-like patio is the ideal place to sit back and relax with their estate grown wines.

BOTTOM LEFT: Winemaker Robbie Meyer looks to tell the story of the estate through a small-lot approach to viticulture and winemaking.

BOTTOM RIGHT: Chef Tony Glanville holds the popular charcuterie board that is made in-house.
Photographs by Ron Essex

THE SPUR

GOURMET PAIRINGS

Vindaloo sliders are the perfect pairing for Murrieta's Well's The Spur. The spices accentuate the earthy notes of the Bordeaux varietals in this red blend, while the tannins from the Petite Sirah help balance the dish by cutting the fat of the lamb.

TASTING NOTES

The Spur is crafted from blending the classic Bordeaux varietals with Petite Sirah, which offers a distinctively California expression. Each varietal is farmed, harvested, and handcrafted individually to achieve the greatest expression. Expect aromas and flavors of vanilla, spiced cranberry, and clove with the perfect balance of graham cracker and plum on the palate followed by assertive tannins and a lasting, elegant mouthfeel.

WINEMAKER'S INSIGHT

All the varietals in this wine's composition were fermented individually at cool temperatures in stainless steel tanks and pumped over three times daily to maintain the full fruit expression of the vineyard.

AWARDS & DISTINCTIONS

The Spur has received 90-plus point ratings from James Suckling, *Wine Spectator, Wine Enthusiast,* Tasting Panel, and Decanter.

TECHNICAL DATA

APPELLATION: Livermore Valley
COMPOSITION: 64% Cabernet Sauvignon, 14% Petite Sirah, 13% Merlot, 9% Petit Verdot
MATURATION: aged for 24 months in 40 percent new, 40 percent second-use, and 20 percent third-use French oak.
CELLARING: It's luscious upon release, and can be cellared for up to six years.

ORDER OUR WINE

Visit our website by scanning the image to left

Nella Terra Cellars LIVERMORE VALLEY

The Beemiller family has owned the Nella Terra Cellars land since 1979, and has always appreciated the beauty of the property. They felt it was so beautiful in fact, that Gerry and Paulette were compelled to share it with the public and decided to plant a vineyard and open their doors. The first vineyard was planted in 2013. They had lived on the property long enough to know that the cool nights, evening winds, and morning fog would be a climate that would lend itself nicely to Pinot Noir. After the vineyard went in the ground, Nella Terra began hosting large private events in 2014, and it's now a multi-generational family owned and operated business.

The vineyard sits in the Sunol Highlands at 1,100 feet and gets a maritime breeze off of the San Francisco Bay, creating a generally cooler climate than the rest of the Livermore Valley AVA. Gerry knew that Pinot Noir would be a difficult crop to grow and understood all of the unknowns, yet he took the risk and never looked back. The first few vintages from the vineyard proved to be a success, aging well in bottle, and subsequent vintages got better each year. The unique micro-climate has proven itself as an ideal setting for outstanding Pinot Noir.

Today, husband-and-wife team of Griffin and Kendall Beemiller run daily planning and operations of the winery and vineyard. They also do a bit of the winemaking and vineyard management, however most of those responsibilities are outsourced to companies within the Livermore Valley, with all resources

FACING PAGE: The view from the top of Nella Terra Cellars' Pinot Noir Vineyard overlooking the event space tucked away in a valley of the Sunol Highlands.

ABOVE: The patio at Nella Terra Cellars is surrounded by beautiful vineyard and garden views.
Photographs by Junshien International

grown on site. In addition to Pinot Noir, they grow Viognier, Petite Sirah, and Primitivo, as well as Syrah, Chardonnay, Sauvignon Blanc, Semillon, and Albariño. Visitors can sip and sample these varietals in the Nella Terra tasting room, where guests are made to feel at home and can always find a family member to chat with. Nella Terra means "into the earth" in Italian, and the cellars have a clear connection to the earth on which they sit. The team is focused on the land and soil, studying the ritual of the vines, and committed to creating quality estate-grown fruit.

TOP: The staircase leading through the Pinot Noir vineyard is made from native stone harvested from the property. Seashell fossils can be found embedded in the rocks.
Photograph by Junshien International

BOTTOM LEFT: Paulette and Gerry Beemiller are the founders and owners of Nella Terra Cellars.
Photograph by Ron Essex

BOTTOM RIGHT: Kendall Beemiller, wine sales and marketing, with husband Griffin Beemiller, wine and vineyard operations.
Photograph by Ron Essex
Photograph by Branded Content Media

NELLA TERRA ESTATE PINOT NOIR

GOURMET PAIRINGS
Pairs with a plate of lamb pastrami, pickled onion, and coffee rye bread, shown here from Salt Craft restaurant in Pleasanton. The lamb lends itself nicely to the acidity and red fruits of the Pinot Noir, bringing forward the complexity of the wine.

TASTING NOTES
This Pinot Noir has balanced acidity with ripe red fruit. It has aromas of pomegranate, cherries, and strawberries with a peppery, dark fruit finish. The wine is dry with medium body and mild tannin. Fruit flavors dominate the palate while the oak influence takes a back seat to the primary fruit flavors.

WINEMAKER'S INSIGHT
Nella Terra is blazing new trails by growing Pinot Noir in the Sunol Highlands, so every year the team learns a little bit more. Its close vicinity to the San Francisco Bay imparts unique climatic effects, such as morning fog and evening wind gusts. This breeze, along with strict canopy management, minimizes the appearance of mildew in the delicate Pinot Noir vineyards. When it comes time to harvest, the small Pinot Noir bunches are hand-picked and whole-berry fermented.

TECHNICAL DATA

APPELLATION: Livermore Valley
COMPOSITION: 100% estate-grown Pinot Noir
MATURATION: The juice is macerated on skins for two weeks, then aged in mostly neutral oak for 18 months.
CELLARING: It can be cellared for five-plus years.

ORDER OUR WINE

Visit our website by scanning the image to left

Omega Road Winery LIVERMORE VALLEY

Before opening Omega Road Winery, Ken Henkelman worked in the wine industry in the late 1960s and early 1970s at Robert Mondavi and Chateau Montelena. He had a degree and got a job in the industry, but Ken's life took a different direction and he walked away from winemaking for many years. Around 2007, he returned to what he loves to do and began making wine in his garage. But it wasn't until his daughter Alexandra returned home from college and joined in her father's passion that the business brainstorming began. They started taking classes together at Las Positas College while continuing to make wine at home. Quickly, they developed a shared love of the craft of winemaking and started making wine under the label Omega Road Winery with one premise: Great wine should bring people together.

Early on, Ken and Alexandra were working out of a small shop in San Ramon on Omega Road, and although they outgrew the space, they kept the name. It's an homage to where they began and keeps them connected to their roots. The winery was officially established in 2011 in the picturesque Livermore Valley, but the tasting room was opened in 2017.

Ken and Alexandra continue to partner daily in the winemaking, with Alexandra also handling events and marketing management. Ken's wife and Alexandra's mom, Nicky, also help run the business. Omega Road offers Torrontes, Verdelho, and Nero d'Avola. Plus, the team produces Viognier, Petit Verdot, Syrah, and more, with most of the grapes sourced from Livermore Valley and a few upcoming varietals from other areas of Northern California.

FACING PAGE: Omega Road Winery is a family business run by dad Ken, daughter Alexandra, and mom Nicky.

ABOVE At Omega Road, we are always ready to open and share a bottle and glass of wine.
Photographs by Ron Essex

179

The family loves sharing their wines with visitors and introducing them to unusual varietals and interesting styles. Tastings are held every Saturday and Sunday in the tasting room on Vasco Road. In addition to visiting the tasting room, guests are welcome to tour the industrial complex, and visit the barrel room, as well. Events and festivals happen year-round, so make sure and check the Omega Road website or call before visiting to see what's in store.

ABOVE: Alexandra Henkelman enjoys a glass of wine in the barrel storage room at Omega Road Winery.

LEFT: The goal at Omega Road Winery is to bring people together through the enjoyment of great wine.
Photographs by Ron Essex

PETIT VERDOT

GOURMET PAIRINGS

A natural fit for rich, meat dishes, grilled steak, spicy pork, veal, lamb, and all types of game and sausage.

TASTING NOTES

Brilliantly complex and fantastically approachable, this stunning varietal highlights baked boysenberry, fresh figs, and a myriad of spices. After taking a sip, seductive cacao and fresh tobacco leaf join the beautiful fruits on the palate, with an extended finish reflecting the essence of the aromas.

WINEMAKER'S INSIGHT

These grapes are a gem of the Livermore Valley. They represent the beauty of the soil, the stunning climate, and the characteristics of the fruit. With this wine, the team did their best to not stand in the way of the grapes and let them shine.

AWARDS & DISTINCTIONS

Gold Medal – Denver International

TECHNICAL DATA

APPELLATION: Livermore Valley
COMPOSITION: 100% Petit Verdot
MATURATION: The wine is aged 30 months in a combination of new and neutral French and American oak.
CELLARING: Fantastic now, and will continue to be delicious for the next three years or so.

ORDER OUR WINE

Visit our website by scanning the image to left

Wente Vineyards LIVERMORE VALLEY

In celebrating its 136th year, Wente Vineyards is America's oldest, continuously owned and operated family winery, now under the management of the family's fourth and fifth generations. Family owned, estate grown and sustainably farmed — that's the Wente philosophy.

The Wente family roots date back to 1883 when German immigrant Carl H. Wente arrived in Livermore, purchased 48 acres of vineyards, and established the eponymous winery. In 1908, his son Ernest Wente obtained Chardonnay cuttings from the Theodore Gier Vineyard in Pleasanton, California, and planted them at the Wente Estate. By 1912, different Chardonnay cuttings were added which came from the F. Richter Nursery in Montpellier, France.

During the Prohibition era, the Wente family stayed in business by making white wine for Napa Valley's Beaulieu Winery, which then sold it as sacramental wine. After the repeal of Prohibition in 1933, the advent of varietal labeling, which Wente Vineyards pioneered, increased the demand for Chardonnay and led Ernest to start selecting vines with the best physiology and flavors to be replicated. Over the next 30 years, Wente's signature cuttings were highly desired by numerous top wineries, many of which still have the clonal material today.

The bowl-shaped Livermore Valley (30 miles east of the San Francisco Bay) is more than 20 miles in length and has numerous microclimates and varied soil types. Wente's estate vineyards are located on sloping hillsides, on ancient

FACING PAGE: Rolling Hills of Wente Vineyards in the Livermore Valley.

ABOVE: The Winemakers Studio at Wente Vineyards allows wine connoisseurs of all levels to blend their very own bottle of wine.
Photographs courtesy of Wente Family Estates

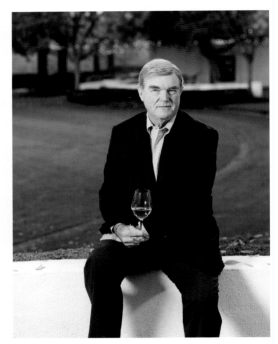
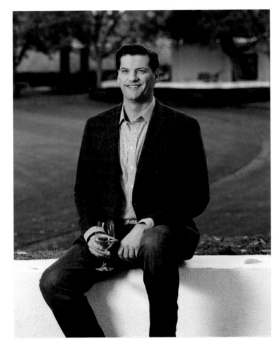
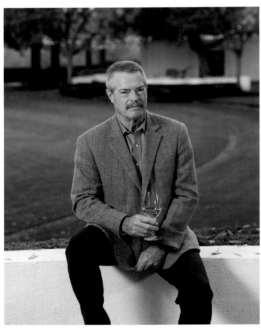

stony riverbeds, along fertile valley floors and at the base of steep sandstone cliffs. Additional vineyards planted with Chardonnay, Riesling, and Pinot Noir are located in Monterey County's Arroyo Seco appellation.

Hailed as one of the top winegrowers and producers in California, Wente Vineyards' portfolio includes more than 40 different wines. These are single-vineyard and estate-grown tiers of wines such as Chardonnay, Cabernet Sauvignon, Merlot, Syrah, Sauvignon Blanc, and some Riesling. There are bold complex blends in the Bordeaux and Rhône styles and varietal bottlings of Zinfandel, Cabernet Franc, and Petite Sirah.

Wine tasting is divided in two locations: the estate winery and visitors center on Tesla Road and at scenic grounds of the Arroyo Road property (the former historic Cresta Blanca Winery) at the terraced vineyard tasting room. Here visitors can enjoy fine

dining and take in a game of golf on the Greg Norman-designed 18-hole course.

A Wente experience offers a variety of tours from wine and cheese pairing in the sandstone caves to private group tastings and tours through the historic property and vineyards. These tours can be booked in advance.

TOP PHOTOS: Left to right: Fourth and fifth generation Winegrowers Carolyn Wente, Eric Wente and Karl D. Wente

BELOW PHOTOS: Left to right: Philip Wente, Niki Wente, Jordan Wente. Not pictured are fifth generation Winegrowers Christine Wente and Aly Wente. *Photographs courtesy of Wente Family Estates*

RIVA RANCH VINEYARD CHARDONNAY

GOURMET PAIRINGS

The creamy balanced acidity of Riva Ranch Chardonnay pairs beautifully with hazelnut-crusted sea bass with chorizo puree, Romanesco, capers, and mussels.

TASTING NOTES

The Riva Ranch Vineyard Chardonnay is a beautifully rich, yet balanced California-style Chardonnay that has aromas of grilled pineapple and graham crackers. This wine has a creamy mouthfeel and a great core of acidity.

WINEMAKER'S INSIGHT

The Chardonnay is sourced exclusively from the Riva Ranch Vineyard in Arroyo Seco, in California's Monterey County. Arroyo Seco—where Wente has been growing grapes since third generation Karl L. Wente purchased the vineyard in 1961—is heaven on earth for the cultivation of Chardonnay. The deep, well-drained gravelly soils and a prevailing cool climate allow for slow and even ripening of this expressive wine.

AWARDS & DISTINCTIONS

93 points, Gold, & Best in Class – Los Angeles international Wine Competition (two-time winner)
96 points, Double Gold – San Francisco International Wine Competition
91 points – Blue Lifestyle, Anthony Dias Blue

TECHNICAL DATA

APPELLATION: Arroyo Seco, Monterey
COMPOSITION: 98% Chardonnay, 2% Gewurztraminer
MATURATION: This wine is aged sur-lie for eight months, where the wine undergoes 100 percent malolactic fermentation.
CELLARING: Enjoy now, or cellar for up to two to three years.

ORDER OUR WINE

Visit our website by scanning the image to left

Blair Estate Wines CARMEL-BY-THE SEA

If you're lucky, you come across a woman like Delfina once in your lifetime. And if you're Jeffrey Blair, you're fortunate enough to have her as a grandmother.

Jeffrey was an unruly child in a family of seven kids and was often sent to stay under the loving eye of his grandmother, who lived just down the road. Encouraging, patient, and always ready to teach Jeffrey something new, Delfina spent most of her time in the kitchen—nothing was more important than food, wine, and family. She never met a stranger and was unanimously loved by the local ranch hands, who were regularly treated to her delicious homemade meals. Iginio, his grandfather, made wine in the cellar while Jeffrey observed with intense interest. It's here that he learned to appreciate all things culinary and began to fall in love with what would become his future: winemaking. Swiss-Italian immigrants, his grandparents came to California in the 1920s and operated a dairy farm with a lush garden and plenty of rabbits, pigs, and other animals that Jeffrey enjoyed as a child. Today that same land is part of Blair Vineyards' "Delfina's Vineyard", sitting among the nearly 10 acres of Pinot Noir and Chardonnay vines.

With Delfina's inspiration in every vintage, Blair Estate produces Pinot Gris, Pinot Noir, Rosé of Pinot Noir, and Chardonnay. Jeffrey subscribes to the philosophy that the vineyards indicate when the grapes are ready, and because of this, the wine has beautiful, unforced flavors. This often means that the fruit takes longer to reach its peak, but the end results are premium flavors, mouthfeel, and composition. The vineyards are set in the northeast corner of the Arroyo Seco AVA—the coldest, windiest place in Monterrey County—and yield dynamic flavors. Cool air from the pristine waters of Monterey Bay blow down the Salinas Valley every afternoon and give the grapes Burgundian qualities and make for

FACING PAGE: Sunrise brings a new day at Delfina's Vineyard, with mounting excitement as another harvest is approaching.
Photograph by Jeffrey Blair

ABOVE: Father-daughter Jeffrey and Mallory Blair tastes the award-winning wines from Delfina's Vineyard. Terroir-expressive Pinot Noirs are the specialty at Blair Estate.
Photograph by Denim & Velvet Marketing + Design

unique wines. Jeffrey leads a team of dedicated vineyard workers who have mastered the art of clipping and pruning the stubborn, sensitive grapes, and helps in every overnight harvest.

Blair Vineyards is the direct result of love and encouragement from Jeffrey's grandmother, and pays homage to the five generations of family who have lived on the land. His no-frills approach gives the wines an honest, timeless flavor that pay no mind to ever-changing trends. If not in the vineyard, Jeffrey can be found in the tasting room, located on the lower level of the Carmel Plaza in downtown Carmel-By-The-Sea.

TOP LEFT: Rosie, the vineyard dog, oversees the development of a new block of clones "DRC", "828" and "943" Pinot Noir vines in Delfina's Vineyard.
Photograph by Jeffrey Blair

BELOW LEFT: Magnums and Double Magnums of award-winning Blair Estate Pinot Noir and Chardonnay.
Photograph by Denim & Velvet Marketing + Design

ABOVE: Often you will find winemaker and owner Jeffrey Blair working in the Carmel-by-the Sea tasting room–a job he thoroughly enjoys.
Photograph by Denim & Velvet Marketing + Design

DELFINA'S VINEYARD PINOT NOIR, "THE RESERVE"

GOURMET PAIRINGS

An incredibly food-versatile Pinot Noir; try it with roast rabbit with rosemary and herbs, served with soft polenta and garden carrots.

TASTING NOTES

In the glass, the signature Delfina's Pinot Noir, "The Reserve" displays aromas of herbs and flavored tea, cherries, and baking spices. The palate has a velvety entry displaying finesse and elegance that a great Pinot can provide. This wine is an experience, offering notes of plum, cherry, tobacco, strawberry, earth, and minerality. It is balanced, and has a smooth finish with sweet tannins and sweet fruit.

WINEMAKER'S INSIGHT

This wine, in true Blair fashion, was made without a refractometer and depended solely on Jeffrey's palate. He selected, in the vineyard, just enough fruit for five barrels worth of truly exceptional Pinot Noir. These were the grapes destined to become The Reserve release. At most, only 125 cases of The Reserve is produced each vintage.

AWARDS & DISTINCTIONS

97 points – The Certified Truth, Steve Pollack
94 points –*Wine Enthusiast*
92 points –International Wine Review
92 points – *Tasting Panel Magazine*
Platinum – Northwest Food & Wine Competition
93 points, Double Gold – American Fine Wine Competition
94 points, Gold – New York International Wine Competition

TECHNICAL DATA

APPELLATION: Arroyo Seco
COMPOSITION: 100 % Pinot Noir
MATURATION: 100 percent new Seguin Moreau and Francois Ferre French oak barrels, 25 percent Puncheons, and 75 percent 60-gallon barrels, and then aged for 14 to15 months.
CELLARING: Phenomenal now but can be cellared for seven to 10 years.

LEARN MORE

Visit our website by scanning the image on the left

BLAIR ESTATE | PINOT NOIR

Signature Wines and Wineries of Coastal California

DeTierra Vineyards CARMEL-BY-THE SEA

De Tierra Vineyards is owned by Dan McDonnal and Alix Lynn Bosch, and their goal is simple: to produce the highest quality hand-crafted, limited-production wines from the unique terroir of Monterey County. De Tierra translates from Italian to mean "of the land," and as the name suggests, De Tierra focuses on providing the best representation of this land. Dan and Alix produce distinct, award-winning, and sustainably harvested wines. Great wines begin in the vineyard, and it is their objective to transform the defining flavors of this terroir into premium wine.

The winery began in 1998 as an organic grape-growing operation in the Salinas Valley by Tom Russell, an agriculture professional from Phoenix, Arizona. He was passionate about wine and farming, and wanted to explore the benefits of organic farming with wine grapes. The site Tom selected for the Russell Vineyard, Corral De Tierra, is situated between Salinas and Carmel Valley, the area that writer John Steinbeck refers to in his book Pastures of Heaven. Dan and Alix have the privilege of carrying on De Tierra's tradition of producing superior boutique wines.

What started as little more than a hobby has blossomed into a thriving artisanal brand with distribution in 22 states, numerous accolades, a thriving wine club, and a burgeoning team of experienced wine enthusiasts at its helm. De Tierra produces nine single varietals: Riesling, Chardonnay, Pinot Noir,

FACING PAGE: The European Café-inspired tasting room in picturesque Carmel-by-the-Sea is warm and inviting with ample seating–and it's dog friendly too.

ABOVE: Morning at the Russell Vineyard, which author John Steinbeck refers to in Pastures of Heaven.
Photographs courtesy of DeTierra Vineyards

191

RUSSELL VINEYARD CABERNET FRANC

GOURMET PAIRINGS

As a medium-bodied wine with high acidity, this wine pairs nicely with duck breast with mustard greens, turnips, and radishes. This dish makes use of the robust tannins with a juicy duck breast as well as highlighting the earthy and herbaceous notes in this wine with mustard greens, turnips, and radishes.

TASTING NOTES

The first thing you will notice is the beautiful deep, red color. Your nose will discover beautiful mineral-driven notes of slate, flint, and river rock. These notes lead to bright fruit notes of cranberry and bright cherry, with a hint of black tea. On the palate you will enjoy gentle, well-integrated tannins with balanced fruit notes of cherry and cranberry that carry through from the nose, leading to strong herbal notes on the finish.

WINEMAKER'S INSIGHT

The Russell Vineyard Cabernet Franc is a small production (50 to 100 cases per year), single vineyard, gold medal award-winning wine that is handcrafted. The vines are hand pruned, the grapes are hand-harvested and fermentation is done in small tanks. The wine is aged solely in oak barrels for a minimum of two full years before release. It has a dedicated following and each release usually sells out within few months.

AWARDS & DISTINCTIONS

94 points, Gold Medal – American Fine Wine Competition

TECHNICAL DATA

APPELLATION: Monterey
COMPOSITION: 100% Russell Vineyard Cabernet Franc
MATURATION: Aged a minimum of 24 months in oak barrels.
CELLARING: Excellent upon release but will only improve with cellaring for up to 10-plus years.

LEARN MORE

Visit our website by scanning the image on left

Merlot, Sangiovese, Syrah, Petit Verdot, Cabernet Sauvignon, and Cabernet Franc, in addition to three red Bordeaux-style blends. All of the wines are crafted with grapes from the original Russell Vineyard and other high-quality vineyards in Monterey County and the surrounding area. Guests are welcome to stop by the cozy European-influenced tasting room in Carmel-by-the-Sea, where they will find large accordion-style windows that open onto Mission Street, bringing in the sunshine and fresh ocean air. Visitors may forget they are in California—the Tasting Room has the distinct feeling of a charming French café.

ABOVE: Sunlight through the Pinot Noir vines in the Russell Vineyard.
Photograph by Steve Zmack

RIGHT: Alix Lynn Bosch and Dan **McDonnal** enjoy some of their wine in the De Tierra Tasting Room.
Photograph courtesy of DeTierra Vineyards

Lightpost Winery MORGAN HILL

Lightpost Winery was established in 2016, but its story began long before that. Lightpost is run by husband-and-wife team John Mauro and Sofia Fedotova, who met online and shared a passion for wine, among other things. After 18 years together, the couple managed to open the operation with the love and support of their four kids, family, and friends, backed by hard work and a strong appreciation for winemaking. Today, they work alongside their award-winning, French-Burgundian winemaker, Christian Roguenant, to showcase European-style wines in their region.

Lightpost is a boutique family winery, set in Morgan Hill, at the southern tip of Silicon Valley (San Francisco Bay Area). The tasting room, housed in the historic building where Thomas Kinkade painted much of his celebrated artwork, is conveniently located right off the Highway 101 exit, providing easy access for residents and visitors. It offers multiple areas to have an unforgettable experience, including a modern tasting room, separate family room, club members' lounge, and a private group and events rooms. In addition to tasting award-winning wines, guests can relax in the outdoor seating area, make a wish under the Lightpost wishing tree, drop a postcard into happy wishes mailbox, and take pictures with interactive wine glass and bottle art sculptures.

The grapes are sourced from Estate Vineyard as well as from carefully selected premium single vineyards along the coastal line of California. Estate Vineyard is comprised of diverse but well-drained soils located in Santa Clara

FACING PAGE: This lush, richly textured, voluptuous Classic Red wine with dark garnet color is powerfully flavored and ideal for everyday celebrations

ABOVE: The grand entry sculpture of wine bottle and wine glass are a perfect picture opportunity.
Photographs by Brandon Stier/Oak & Barrel Photography

PINOT NOIR, SANTA CRUZ MOUNTAINS, FERRARI VINEYARDS

GOURMET PAIRINGS
Pair with sautéed Alaskan halibut topped with wild mushrooms and served with a reduction sauce made with capers.

TASTING NOTES
This powerfully flavored, deep ruby-colored, full-bodied, and concentrated Pinot Noir has expressions of fruit, floral, plums, red and black cherry, boysenberry, cracked pepper, earth tones, and spice. It is well balanced with integrated acidity, structured tannin, and hints of vanilla from lots of French oak barrels. Compelling in every way, it offers hints of juicy raspberry fruit that's focused, pure, and undeniably delicious.

WINEMAKER'S INSIGHT
This three-acre vineyard is located in the cool Corralito's hills, four-and-a-half miles from the Pacific Ocean. Surrounded by large redwood trees, this 35-year-old vineyard is farmed organically and without irrigation. Following three days of cold soak, the wine ferments on its skins for three weeks in one-and-a-half-ton bins and is hand-punched down several times a day.

AWARDS & DISTINCTIONS
The wine has won numerous gold medals at wine competitions.

TECHNICAL DATA

APPELLATION: Santa Cruz Mountains
COMPOSITION: 10% Pinot Noir
MATURATION: Aged 10 months in 50 percent French oak barrel from Central France.
CELLARING: This very complex wine is delicious now but would benefit to be cellared for a decade to explore another dimension and show its full potential.

LEARN MORE

Visit our website by scanning image on left.

Valley, and is the state's first premiere wine-production region with a winemaking history that dates back to 1777. Today, the Lightpost portfolio focuses on exploring the endless potential of the diverse growing conditions that the best Central Coast vineyards offer. The winery draws from tradition but embraces the future, and utilizes the unique gifts from the earth to craft wines that are a true representation of each terroir—all while featuring Christian's distinct winemaking skills that won him Winemaker of the Year in San Luis Obispo County.

Lightpost Winery is poised to bring exceptional wines and engaging experiences to locals and visitors. Single-varietal wines, Rhône, and Bordeaux-style blends are created in limited lots, displaying exquisite varietal character. It includes voluptuous full-bodied Cabernet Sauvignon with deep lush color; power-flavored and elegant Pinot Noirs; European-style Chardonnay with mineral-fresh notes; and smooth and rich Chardonnay. The tantalizing trio of white Rhône varietals features Marsanne, Rousanne, and Grenache Blanc. The Albariño has plenty of minerality and freshness on the palate, accompanied by elegant and seductive sparkling wines.

Within its production, the winery features three tiers of wine, offered under two different presentations. Premium category wines featuring Mr. and Mrs. Lightpost are fun, festive, and ready for everyday celebrations, but also worth cellaring. Reserve Wines come in traditional, elegant packaging, made from special sites with additional aging, exclusively stored in

French oak barrels. The Burgundy tier expresses the beauty of Chardonnay and Pinot Noir grown in the cool climate of Santa Cruz Mountains, Santa Lucia Highlands, Edna Valley, and Santa Rita Hills. The Bordeaux tier celebrates the classic and traditional style of western Southern France and the joys of adventure with its collection of blends of single vineyards from West Paso Robles, Santa Clara Valley, and Santa Cruz Mountains. The Rhône tier represents the pioneering spirit of small-lot wines made from Syrah and Grenache grapes grown in the Paso Robles and Santa Clara Valley region.

Unique tasting experiences that showcase the decadent fruit of Santa Clara Valley and Central Coast cool-climate vineyards make it a must-visit winery destination.

TOP LEFT: Lightpost Winery glass of wine... deliciousness awaits!

TOP RIGHT: Lightpost team: (left to right)American-Russian-French trio (John Mauro, Sofia Fedotova andChristian Roguenant).
Photographs by Brandon Stier/Oak & Barrel Photography

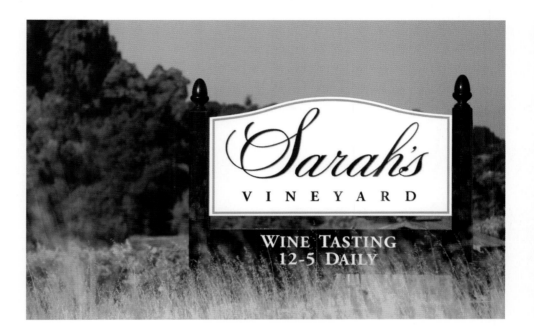

Sarah's Vineyard GILROY

The Sarah's Vineyard estate is a labor of love for winegrower Tim Slater. Tim took the helm at Sarah's Vineyard when he purchased the vineyards and winery in 2001. Prior to that, Tim explored many career paths, including being a DJ, a musician, and a successful micro-machining engineer with a number of patents. He brought a scientific approach to replanting and modernizing Sarah's, finely balanced by an artist's sensibility and a traditionalist's love of the land.

By channeling both his inner mad scientist and his artistic side, the estate has flourished, growing and producing some of California's finest Pinot Noir and Chardonnay. "My philosophy is a fairly simple one," says Tim, "bottle by bottle, vintage by vintage, to capture the 'music of the vineyard.'"

As a hands-on proprietor, Tim is both grower and winemaker, constantly experimenting in the vineyard and in the cellar. He can also be found in the tasting room, sharing his latest discoveries with guests. The Sarah's Vineyard estate occupies 28 acres in the cool climate of the Mount Madonna foothills of the southern Santa Cruz Mountain range. Here, chilling winds and fog from Monterey Bay mitigate the sunny daytime temperatures and extend hang time, creating perfect conditions for growing world-class Pinot Noir and Chardonnay.

Sarah's is made up of three main vineyard blocks: the original Sarah's Vineyard plantings that date back to 1978, plus the newer Timcat and Dwarf Oak sections. And while the Burgundian varieties may be Sarah's claim to fame,

FACING PAGE: Looking south from Sarah's Vineyard into the Mount Madonna Foothills of the southern Santa Cruz Mountains.

ABOVE: Sarah's Vineyard entrance off of Hecker Pass Highway in Gilroy.
Photographs courtesy Sarah's Vineyard

Tim also cultivates his interest in the traditional Rhône grapes with several blocks planted to Grenache, Viognier, Roussanne, Grenache Blanc, Piquepoul Blanc, Clairette Blanche, Mourvèdre, and Counoise. What's Tim's secret to great winemaking? Ideal climate and soils paired to a single-minded obsession with quality. Tim exercises complete control of the process "from the dirt to the bottle" for the winery's Dwarf Oak, Estate, Appellation, and Reserve series wines. That passion and dedication has led to Sarah's being awarded numerous 90-plus scores from the likes of *Wine Spectator Magazine*.

Sarah's Vineyard is also one of the Central Coast's most popular visitor destinations. The tasting room is open daily for sampling just minutes from the hustle and bustle of Silicon Valley; it has become a must-stop spot on any Pinot Noir fan's itinerary.

Warm hospitality, vineyard views, and exceptional wines—many only available here, at the source—make for a memorable winery experience. The tasting room hosts a popular summer music series and is home base for Sarah's Vineyard wine club members, who receive first access to Tim's limited releases.

TOP LEFT: Among the vine rows at Sarah's Vineyard.

TOP RIGHT: Tim and Megan admire the scenery at Sarah's Vineyard along with winery dog, Draco.

BELOW LEFT: Sarah's Vineyard's outdoor stage is the site for its popular music series.

BELOW RIGHT: Tim is often to be found personally hosting guests in Sarah's tasting room west of Gilroy.
Photographs courtesy Sarah's Vineyard

SARAH'S VINEYARD PINOT NOIR RESERVE

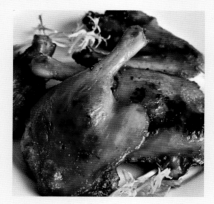

GOURMET PAIRINGS

The Sarah's Vineyard Reserve Pinot Noir's rich cherry and plum flavors, and savory character, are a match made in heaven with the umami elements of a dish such as crispy Asian duck confit with soy sauce egg and black rice.

TASTING NOTES

The black-labeled flagship Reserve Pinot Noir is a special wine. Tim Slater typically makes less than 200 cases of this beauty in a vintage. The Santa Clara Valley is a storied winegrowing district, stretching back to the early 1850s, perhaps best known for "bigger" reds. But Sarah's Vineyard's location in the appellation is a unique one. A gap in the Mount Madonna foothills funnels breezes and evening fog directly into the S.V. vines, providing superior climatic conditions for growing superb Pinot Noir.

WINEMAKER'S INSIGHT

"We gently destem whole berries into small fermenters, cold soak for three days, allowing a robust native fermentation, then inoculate with RC212 yeast to ensure complete fermentation. We hand-punch down three times daily. The wine is pressed off the skins when the RS is below 20 grams of sugar per liter, and fermentation is completed in barrel. The wine is bottled and labeled with a hand-waxed capsule; it is allowed a year of bottle age prior to release."

AWARDS & DISTINCTIONS

This wine consistently receives 90-plus point scores from *Wine Spectator* and other leading wine industry reviewers.

TECHNICAL DATA

APPELLATION: Santa Clara Valley
COMPOSITION: 100% Pinot Noir, primarily Dijon clones 667 and 777 from our Dwarf Oak blocks.
MATURATION: The cooperage used is typically François Frères and Vallaurine, 33 percent new oak with the balance in one- and two-year old barrels. Barrel maturation is approximately 18 months.
CELLARING: Drinks well upon release; will reward proper cellaring for 10 years from vintage date.

ORDER OUR WINE

Most Sarah's Vineyard wines are limited releases. Please visit our website for availability by scanning the image on the left.

Solis Winery GILROY

Solis Winery is tucked away in the far southwest corner of Santa Clara Valley—one of the oldest commercial wine regions in California. The Solis story begins with the Bertero family, who owned and operated a winery on the same site in the early 1900s. Alfonso Bertero planted the vineyard and built a house in 1922, which is the same home that visitors see today when they approach the winery. The home has a distinct, crushed abalone shell exterior, one of only two homes with this feature in Santa Clara County. Alfonso operated his winery until the 1980s—even through Prohibition as a bootlegger—until it was purchased by investors.

By this time, Dave Vanni and his family had moved next door to the winery on a five-acre vineyard. Although the investors struggled to keep the winery afloat, it eventually fell into foreclosure. The Vannis saw an opportunity and purchased the neighboring land in 1989 and gave it the full name of Rancho de Solis Winery. The Vannis had been acquiring several nearby parcels and replanted the old vineyards with Chardonnay and Merlot, adding new state-of-the-art trellis systems and irrigation.

When Dave procured the winery, winemaking was just a hobby, but with the help of his wife Valerie, it became a full-time job. They began to redefine the entire region by using new technology, focused marketing, and planting new and upcoming varietals. For the next 15 years, they continued to win prestigious awards, increase production, and improve wine quality.

FACING PAGE: A view of the Gabilan mountains and the 30-year-old vines at the Solis estate vineyard.

ABOVE: Owners, Vic and Mike Vanni in the Solis Winery wine cellar.
Photographs by Steve Forman

FIANO

GOURMET PAIRINGS

Pair this wine with crab cakes, grilled scallops, pineapple fried rice, and dishes with champagne vinaigrette dressing, or drink on its own.

TASTING NOTES

The Fiano grape is indigenous to Southern Italy and produces this lovely, clean, refreshing varietal. It's crisp and refreshing with fresh lemon and lychee on the nose. Pineapple and grapefruit shine on the palate with a bright minerality. Notes of lemongrass and a touch of white pepper add complexity.

WINEMAKER'S INSIGHT

The Fiano is hand-picked in the morning while the grapes are cold. We start pressing immediately and begin a slow, controlled fermentation in stainless steel tanks.

AWARDS & DISTINCTIONS

Double Gold Medal – Central Coast Wine Competition
Best of Show – Central Coast Wine Competition
Gold Medal – Critics Challenge Wine Competition

TECHNICAL DATA

APPELLATION: Santa Clara Valley
COMPOSITION: 100% estate-grown Fiano
MATURATION: Aged five months in a stainless-steel tank. No oak barrel aging, and malolactic fermentation is minimalized to maintain acidity.
CELLARING: This wine drinks beautifully now and do so for the next few years.

LEARN MORE

Visit our website by scanning image on left

In 2000, Dave's son Mike joined the family winery and apprenticed under the winemaker at the time. Then, in 2007, Dave and Valerie decided to retire, handing the winery to both Mike and his brother ,Vic, who operate the winery together today. Mike handles all the vineyards and winemaking, and continues to produce consistently well-valued, high-quality wines, even winning Best Merlot in the entire state at the California State Fair Wine Competition. Vic oversees the business and marketing end of the operation.

Solis Winery has become well-known for most of its red estate varietal wines including Syrah, Sangiovese, Zinfandel, and Merlot, but also has a great reputation for the three blends: Baciami, Cara Mia, and Seducente. Also, Solis Winery is one of the few wineries in the state to grow and produce Fiano, an Italian white varietal. The winery is ideal to visit year-round and hosts events such as Cigars Under the Stars, Cab & Kabobs, and Member-Guest Barrel Tasting. Call the winery or head to the website for more details.

TOP LEFT & RIGHT: Owners, Mike and Vic would love to pour you a glass of their Bourdeaux blend, "Cara Mia" and other fine estate wines when you visit Solis Winery.

BELOW: The view of the outdoor tasting area and the Vanni Estate Vineyard in Gilroy from the Solis Winery patio.
Photographs by Steve Forman

Wineries You Need To Visit on California's Central Coast

Adelaida Cellars
5805 Adelaida Road
Paso Robles, CA 93446
805.239.8980

Aleksander Wine   13
5885 Vista Del Paso Road
Paso Robles, CA 93446
aleksanderwine.com
310.804.0516
Wine tastings available by invitation
and to members only

Allegretto Vineyard Resort   19
2700 Buena Vista Drive
Paso Robles, CA 93446
805.369.2500
allegrettovineyardresort.com

Allegretto Wines   19
West Side Tasting Room
6996 Peachy Canyon Road
Paso Robles, CA 93446
805.369.2526
allegrettowines.com
Open: Wed - Sat, noon - 6:45pm
Sun - Mon, 2pm - 6:45pm
Tues by reservation only

Alma Rosa Winery & Vineyards
7250 Santa Rosa Road
Buellton, CA 93427
805.688.9090

Arcadian Winery
1515-B East Chestnut Ave
Lompoc, CA 93436
805.737.3900

Armitage Wines
705 Canham Road
Scotts Valley, CA 95066
831.708.2874

Austin Hope Winery
1585 Live Oak Road
Paso Robles, CA 93446
805.238.4112

Baileyana Winery
5828 Orcutt Road
San Luis Obispo, CA 93401
805.269.8200

Big Basin Vineyards
14598 Big Basin Way
Saratoga , CA 95070
408.564.7346

Big White House Winery   153
   & John Evan Cellars
6800 Greenville Road
Livermore, CA 94550
BigWhiteHouse.com
925.449.1976
Open: Fri-Sun, noon-4:30pm

Blair Estate Vineyards   187
Carmel Plaza, Lower Level
Carmel-by-the-Sea, CA 93921
831.625.WINE (9463)
blairwines.com
Sunday-Thursday, 11am-6pm
Friday-Saturday, 11am-7pm

Brecon Estate Winery   29
7450 Vineyard Drive
Paso Robles, CA 93446
805.239.2200
breconestate.com
Open daily, 11am to 5pm,
tours by appointment

Brian Benson Cellars
2915 Limestone Way
Paso Robles, CA 93446
805.296.9463

Bridlewood Estate Winery
3555 Roblar Avenue
Santa Ynez, CA 93460
800.467.4100

Brochelle Vineyards   31
2323 Tuley Court #130
Paso Robles, CA 93446
brochelle.com
805.237.4410
Open daily, 11am-5pm,
Fri and Sat, 11am-5:30pm

Calera Wine Company
11300 Cienega Road
Hollister, CA 95023
831.637.9170

CaliPaso Winery   37
4230 Buena Vista Drive
Paso Robles, CA 93446
calipasowinery.com
805.226.9296
Open daily, 12pm–7:30pm
Sat – Sun, 1pm–5pm
or by appointment

Concannon Vineyard
4590 Tesla Road
Livermore, CA 94550
925456.2502

Daou Vineyards
2777 Hidden Mountain Road
Paso Robles, CA 93446
888.527.6455

Cooper-Garrod Estate Vineyards   133
22645 Garrod Road
Saratoga, CA 95070
408.867.7116
cgv.com
Open weekdays noon-5pm,
weekends 11am-5pm

Cuda Ridge Wines   159
2400 Arroyo Road
Livermore, CA 94550
510.304.0914
CudaRidgeWines.com
Open: Fri-Sun, noon-4:30 pm

Dante Robere Vineyards   163
1200 Wetmore Road
Livermore, CA 94550
925.245.0172
danterobere.com
Open Friday, 1-pm
Sat and Sun, 12-5pm

Daou Vineyards
2777 Hidden Mountain Road
Paso Robles, CA 93446
888.527.6455

Darcie Kent Vineyards
7000 Tesla Road
Livermore, CA 94550
925.583.1552

David Bruce Winery
21439 Bear Creek Road
Los Gatos, CA 95033
408.354.4214

Derby Wine Estates   47
525 Riverside Drive
Paso Robles, CA 93446
805.238.6300
derbywineestates.com
Open daily 11am-5pm (winter)
11am-6 pm (summer)

De Tierra Vineyards   191
Mission St and 5th Avenue
Carmel-By-The-Sea, CA 93921
831.622.9704
detierra.com
Open Mon– Thur, 2pm-8pm
Fri-Sun, 12pm-8pm

Donati Family Vineyard   55
2720 Oak View Road
Templeton, CA 93465
Donatiwine.com
805.238.0676
Open daily, 11am-5pm

Eberle Winery
3810 Highway 46 East
Paso Robles, CA 93446
805.238.9607

Écluse Wines   61
1520 Kiler Canyon Road
Paso Robles, CA 93446
eclusewines.com
805.238-4999
Open: Fri-Sun, 11am to 4pm
Reservations required for groups

Seven Angels Cellars, page 103

Wineries You Need To Visit on California's Central Coast

Pear Valley Vineyard & Winery
4900 Union Road
Paso Robles, CA 93446
805.237.2861

Pierce Ranch Vineyards
499 Wave Street
Monterey, CA 93940
831.372.8900

Pomar Junction Vineyard & Winery   93
2550 Crested Ridge Lane
Paso Robles, CA 93446
PomarJunction.com
805.238.9940
Private tastings appointment only

Ranchita Canyon Vineyard
3439 Ranchita Canyon Road
San Miguel, CA 93451
805.467.9448

Rancho Sisquoc Winery
6600 Foxen Canyon Road
Santa Maria, CA 93454
805.934.4332

Red Soles Winery & Distillery   99
3230 Oakdale Road
Paso Robles, CA 93446
RedSolesWinery.com
805.226.9898
Open daily, 11am-5pm

Regale Winery
24040 Summit Road
Los Gatos, CA 95033
.408.867.3233

Ridge Vineyards
17100 Montebello Road
Cupertino, CA 95014
408.867.3233

Robert Hall Winery
3443 Mill Road
Paso Robles, CA 93446
805.239.1616

Robert Talbott Vineyards
53 West Carmel Valley Road
Carmel Valley, CA 93924
.831.675.3000

Sanford Winery   141
3230 Oakdale Road
Paso Robles, CA 93446
RedSolesWinery.com
805.226.9898
Open daily, 11am-5pm

Sarah's Vineyard   199
4005 Hecker Pass Hwy
Gilroy, CA 95020
sarahsvineyard.com
408.847.1947
Open daily, 12-5 pm

Satori Cellars
2100 Buena Vista Avenue
Gilroy, CA 95020
408.848.5823

Sculpterra Winery
5015 Linne Road
Paso Robles, CA 93446
805.226.8881

Seven Angels Cellars   103
830 Templeton Road
Templeton, CA 93465
Sevenangelscellars.com
805.835.4054
Call the winery for hours

Seven Oxen Estate Wines   109
3340 Ramada Dr, Ste A
Paso Robles, CA 93446
805.369.2710
sevenoxen.com
Mon 11am-5 pm, Thurs by appt.

Schied Vineyards
1972 Hobson Ave
Greenfield, CA 93927
831.386.0316

Silver Horse Vineyard and Winery
2995 Pleasant Road
San Miguel, CA 93451
805.467.WINE (9463)

Solis Winery   203
3920 Hecker Pass Highway
Gilroy, CA 95020
408.847.6306
soliswinery.com
Open daily, 12-5 pm

Soquel Vineyards
8063 Glen Haven Road
Soquel, CA 95073
831.462.9045

Steinbeck Vineyards & Winery
5940 Union Road
Paso Robles, CA 93446
805.238.1854

Summerwood Winery and Inn
2175 Arbor Road
Paso Robles, CA 93446
805.227.1365

Sycamore Creek Vineyards
12775 Uvas Road
Morgan Hill, CA 95037
408.779.4738

Tablas Creek Vineyard   115
9339 Adelaida Road
Paso Robles, CA 93446
tablascreek.com
805.237.1231
Open daily, 10am-5pm

Talbott Vineyards
53 West Carmel Valley Road
Carmel Valley, CA 93924
831.659.3500

Talley Vineyards
3031 Lopez Drive
Arroyo Grande, CA 93420
805.489.0446

Thomas Fogarty Winery & Vineyard
19501 Skyline Boulevard
Woodside, CA 94062
650.851.6777

Tobin James
8950 Union Rd
Paso Robles, CA 93446
805.239.2204

Toccata
1665 Copenhagen Dr
Solvang CA 93463
805.686.5506

Treana Winery and Hope Family Wines
1585 Live Oak Road
Paso Robles, CA 93447
805.238.4112

Turley Wine Cellars
2900 Vineyard Drive
Templeton, CA 93465
805.434.1030

Villa San-Juliette Vineyard   117
and Winery
6385 Cross Canyons Road
San Miguel, CA 93451
villasanjuliette.com
805.467.0014
Hours: Thur-Mon, 11am-5pm,
by appointment Tues & Wed

Vina Robles   125
3700 Mill Road
Paso Robles, CA 93446
vinarobles.com
805.227.4812
Open daily, 10am-5pm
(hours extended during summer)

Vincent Vineyards   147
2370 N Refugio Road
Santa Ynez, CA 93460
805.691.4200
vincentvineyards.com
Open daily 12-5pm

Wente Vineyards   183
5565 Tesla Road
Livermore, CA 94550
wentevineyards.com
925.456.2305
Open daily 11am-5:30pm

Windward Vineyard   129
1380 Live Oak Road
Paso Robles, CA 93446
805.239.2565
windwardvineyard.com
Open daily 10.30am-5pm

Wrath Winery
35801 Foothill Road
Soledad, CA 93960
831.678.2212

Photograph by Adriana Neal for Seven Oxen Winery, page 109